To Paula
With Love
From Ruth

Here is my brother's first book!

D1304391

WHEN THE CHURCH
LEAVES THE BUILDING

WHEN THE CHURCH LEAVES THE BUILDING

A STORY OF A PEOPLE WHO FOLLOWED THEIR PASSION
WHERE THEY LEAST EXPECTED IT TO TAKE THEM

DAVID FREDRICKSON

COPYRIGHT

Printed in the United States of America

Published by WingSpan Press, Livermore, CA

www.wingspanpress.com

The WingSpan name, logo and colophon are the trademarks of WingSpan Publishing.

EAN 978-1-59594-079-7

ISBN 1-59594-079-0

First Edition 2006

Library of Congress Control Number: 2006930320

Contents

Dedications

To my lovely and very understanding wife, Rachel, who has faithfully stood beside me through rough waters and whose generous heart has helped me to see more of Father's love.

Also, this book would not have been written but for a very flexible and forgiving company of pioneers who have continued to support and love one another while leaving a familiar country to journey into the unknown. This, then, is their story and a tribute to my courageous companions.

Acknowledgements

There are several people who have played an important role in helping me fine tune the manuscript with their suggestions and editing skills. I want to thank Wayne Jacobsen for his valuable input regarding content and for helping to edit the manuscript. Even more significant has been his friendship and encouragement to me personally and to the folks with whom I share this journey.

Special thanks to my sister, Ruth Peters, who gave me her beautiful lakeside condominium for two weeks so that I could finish the book without distractions. She also combed through every page applying her expertise as a writer towards the areas that needed to be polished up a bit.

Thank you, Sue Warren, for correcting punctuation page by page and for offering valuable input in several areas.

Bob Humphrey, my faithful friend and co-worker, spent hours on the computer formatting the manuscript to prepare it for the publisher. Thanks, Bob, for rescuing your technically challenged friend.

Foreword

This book is a treasure—one that will thrill you with each unfolding page! It is the story of a man and congregation that valued God's life above their own experience and the amazing journey that led them to undertake.

Over the course of years, following the gentle nudging of the Spirit, they set out to unravel the mysteries of the body of Christ and found it leading them to places they had never considered. At each turn they continued to risk the status quo and their own comfort and security to find a richer life in Jesus together. They discovered what most people only dare to dream. You'll be shocked at the choices they made and inspired by the lessons they learned.

It is a compelling journal and you will find David's word's raw and honest. This is not the story of a well-constructed success strategy and how to implement it, but of a people willing to go on a journey even though they could only see one step at a time and whose destination was far from clear. The costs were considerable, the rewards far greater.

In the end, whether you agree or disagree with David's choices and conclusions you will know that he has taken the road less traveled—not for his comfort or ego but to follow an undeniable passion deeply planted in his heart. He put it all on the line, even his own vocation; while some of his colleagues did everything they could to dissuade him.

I had the incredible joy of coming alongside these people in the latter stages of their journey and count many of the people you'll read about as close friends. This really happened. I found myself rooting for them and weeping with them as David recounts the joys and challenges of rethinking their life together as the church. It not only transformed them personally, but also taught them how to live freely as the body of Christ every day, not just on Sundays.

At a time when many are rethinking the nature of the body of Christ in the world, this book provides much-needed insight and a powerful example. If you've ever thought that there must be more to church life than going to a building on Sunday mornings, clear your evening. You might be going to sleep a lot later tonight than you planned.

Wayne Jacobsen

lifestream.org

Moorpark, California

Introduction

The story recounted in the pages of this book chronicles the journey of a fellowship of believers who became dissatisfied with "church as usual." They believed that God had a better plan for His family than merely attending meetings and trying to make it through another week between Sundays. As they began to re-examine the scriptures together they discovered that often what they read was very different than what they had been taught or had simply assumed. And the fresh understanding of truth being made real to them was bringing a new-found sense of freedom as well as a greater capacity to receive and give the Father's love.

These discoveries began to change their understanding of what "church" is and how it should function. They became more concerned with *being* the church than attending it or finding a new way to "do" it. New light was shed on why the stories recorded in the book of Acts seemed like a fairy tale compared with the sad reports of the problem-riddled institution of today.

In fact few sincere followers of Christ would deny that the church of today is in serious trouble. The divorce rate within it has skyrocketed and Christian homes produce 79 percent of all alcoholics. Pornography is rampant among pastors. Only 6 to 10 percent of all believers pray and read the word on any regular basis.

In light of these and many other alarming statistics it should not come as a surprise to learn that there has been no church growth in any county in the United States for over a decade. A recent poll revealed that nearly 50 percent of all *committed* Christians are no longer attending church. Many leaders are trumpeting the warning that the church will soon be extinct unless she becomes relevant to the culture she's trying to reach.

I cannot disagree with that assessment in the context of what they are referring to as "church". Both the Christian "drop outs" and most unbelievers as well will tell you that church does not reach them where they live. But I am convinced that not even a reformation will resolve the unhealthy and largely ineffectual condition of the present system. I believe that Jesus intended for the expression and function of His earthly family to be profoundly simple and altogether different than what we call "church" today.

This small book is not intended to be an exhaustive study of principles that will prove to be the key towards reversing the destructive trends mentioned above. Rather, it is the story of one group of people who set out on a spiritual journey in hopes of rediscovering the simple truths that caused the early church to flourish.

The observations made throughout the following pages are not intended to discredit anyone or to diminish the sincere efforts of those who labor faithfully among the people they feel led to serve. Though the validity and virtue of the church system is being challenged here, it must be understood that I do not mean to indict the people within it. The God-loving, fruit-producing men, women and young people who serve Him through an institutional framework most certainly are a joy to the heart of Father. What is shared throughout this writing is intended to motivate the reader to re-evaluate some of the things he or she may believe concerning life in Father's family in light of a fresh re-examination of the Scriptures. It is my hope and prayer that, in so doing, the reader will open the door to greater freedom, love and fruitfulness in his or her own life.

1

STOP THE REVIVAL; GIVE ME THE REAL THING!

The NO TRESPASSING sign was all I needed. Standing in a box canyon at the end of a quarter mile dry creek, staring at a waterfall along with a dozen tourists, was not my idea of adventure. It was about 10:00 in the morning. My wife, Rachel and her friend, Penny would not return to fetch me until early that afternoon. With three hours to kill and no transportation, I decided to make the most of it. The banks of the canyon were overgrown with the lush, green foliage that dominates the landscape in this Hawaiian rain forest. I paused for just a moment to consider the disadvantages of a steep climb through the jungle in my attire, a tank top, shorts and flip flops. A large leather case full of camera equipment dangled from my neck. The sign signaled the challenge, and off I went with the delicious anticipation of an explorer about to encounter the great and dangerous unknown. The terrain grew steeper and the challenge stiffer as I sought footholds and vines to propel and pull myself up the ever-beckoning cliff. Finally, I reached a level area where a narrow path wound its way through mountain apple trees and dense undergrowth. It ended abruptly at a sheer cliff, about 12 feet high. Hanging from the top was a thick rope. *Ah! This was good!* Hand-over-hand I pulled myself upward while the camera case swung back and forth and bounced off my hips. Scrambling over the top, I could hear the distant roar of cascading water and knew I would soon be at the top of the falls.

It was an awe-inspiring sight. From my lofty perch at the mouth of the falls I stared at the endless expanse of turquoise ocean dwarfing the toy-like buildings of Honolulu far below me. Hidden from my view by another mountain was the leeward side of Oahu where the native Hawaiians lived in stark contrast to the frantic bustle of the city. They would be mending their fishing nets outside of humble dwellings on the hillside. Or perhaps they would be patiently waiting for a catch at the edge of the clear waters while children swam in the warm currents or frolicked on the sandy beach.

I finally tore my gaze from the captivating scenery and turned to survey the trail ahead. My eyes followed the path to a section where it cut into the side of the cliff carved from the mountainside by the raging waterfall. Arriving at that point, my left shoulder brushed against the steep embankment rising from the edge of the two foot wide path beneath my feet. On my right was a sheer drop to the base of the canyon hundreds of feet below.

A Frightening Predicament

I had come this far banking on the presupposition that the trail would lead me around the falls and back down to the floor of the canyon. Having observed during the ascent that the lack of footholds on steep embankments would most likely make it impossible to descend, I assumed that this was a one way trail. What I now saw before me made my heart skip a beat. About four feet of the path was completely gone, washed out, no doubt, by heavy rains. Beyond the washout, the path was hard but surfaced in sand and sloped to the edge of the drop-off at a 20 degree angle. Not a promising landing spot. Panic began to shorten my breath and knot my stomach as I considered the options. Attempting to leap across the missing section of path to land upon the angled, sandy surface would most likely send me plummeting hundreds of feet to my death at the bottom of the falls. Yet I was almost certain that the cliffs I had scaled on the way up provided no way down. Suddenly, the path that had offered such stimulating challenges and delightful vistas seemed to cut me off from my goal while making the potential for retreat costly and dangerous.

* * *

The "ministry" path I had traveled over the last 24 years left me in a similar predicament. When first answering the call to "full time" service at 26 years of age, I was full of zeal and vision, anticipating great things ahead. I planned to explore spiritual vistas that were unknown since the days of the early church. I dreamed of leading a company of front-liners from the lowlands of mediocre Christianity to lofty heights where the rarified air had been breathed by the spiritual giants of yesteryear. Each challenge was merely an opportunity to flex my spiritual muscles; each obstacle but a headwind lifting the ministry plane to greater heights.

But after ministering in San Jose, California for 14 years and then in the Sacramento area for the past 10, I realized that the goals and vision I so passionately embraced no longer seemed possible. A decade of zealous preaching, intense discipling, compassionate counseling and creative outreach evangelism had failed to produce an on-fire army of sold out followers of Jesus ready to take the world for Christ. I would often return from ministering overseas with new enthusiasm only to despair at the contrast between the commitment and passion of third world Christians with the apathy and self-centeredness characterizing so many of those I labored amongst at home. Yet after ministering in over a dozen countries, I was forced to admit that even many I worked with in the persecuted church seemed to disappoint my expectations. Sometimes I felt that I was being flattered as a potential source of U.S. dollars. Great emphasis was placed on buildings (except in the underground church of China) and the need for more money. Many seemed overly dependent on the "senior pastor" who "ran" the whole show. The "average Joe" attended meetings hoping to receive a special prayer or touch from the leader, or better yet, from the foreign minister. Often, people would say what they thought I wanted to hear, which would turn out to be opposite of the truth.

Wake-up Call

Back at home the most troubling of all was the lack of love flowing among the members of the body. Day after day I prayed for God's love to grow and flourish anew in our hearts, yet gossip and backbiting continued. My prayers, sermons and counseling seemed to make little difference. Why didn't God come through?

I will never forget the first time I "lost it" while halfway through a sermon. For weeks I had been reading through Isaiah and Jeremiah. One day I told the Lord that I was not getting anything out of the repetitious account of Israel's cycle of idolatry, warnings from God and finally, judgment. I couldn't relate to their gross sins. God's dealings with them seemed predictable. What was supposed to be learned by these gloomy, redundant passages? Suddenly, the unwelcome truth began to dawn on me as though the beam of a searchlight had penetrated my soul.

It seemed that the Holy Spirit was bringing to mind my own self-centeredness. It became painfully clear how often I had indulged my own desires without considering what Father's might be. I had often dictated my own schedule rather than choosing to take His hand and letting Him lead me through each day. I was blind to the self-love and hidden agendas that I had designed to protect my image and thus "save my life." Self was my idol. I remembered that God had called Israel the "apple of his eye." If he had spoken such things to them, why would he not address me just as severely?

Humbled, I began to confess my sin as the Holy Spirit brought conviction and worked to bring me to a place of repentance. In my arrogance, I thought that because I had quit watching TV, did not attend movies, and tried to keep myself from any other "contaminants," I was above such indictments. Gently, the Holy Spirit revealed my self righteousness and desperate need for God's grace. I was reminded of Jesus' words when on one occasion He condemned the Pharisees for their hypocrisy. "You clean the outside of the cup and dish," He said, "but inside they are full of greed and self-indulgence. Blind Pharisee! First clean the inside of the cup and dish, and then the outside also will be clean." It seemed that the higher I raised the standard for myself and for others, the more critical and unloving I became. I had mistaken my own concept of "right doing" for the righteousness that can only come from the faith of Christ who has already finished the work. I had used my will power to clean up the outside while my heart remained proud and selfish. It began to dawn on me that the many hours I had spent in prayer and Bible study, the strict disciplines I adhered to, and the "sacrifices" I had made to serve God were all dead works without love. And love was not something I could produce. I could only ask Father, by His grace, to change my heart.

After a season of repentance and reflection, I sensed the Holy Spirit beginning to draw my focus away from my own condition to that of those I ministered to. Once more, the severe words God had spoken to Israel and had now applied to my own life were brought to mind. I could not shake the strong impression that God was asking me to share this same message to the congregation I addressed every Sunday. This was a chilling thought. I had never heard any preacher deliver such harsh sounding words to a congregation of well-meaning people. As the days went by, I found myself heavily burdened for the church at large. It seemed as though the Holy Spirit was groaning and weeping through me over the condition of the bride of Christ.

Revival at Last?

It was on a Sunday morning at the Seventh Day Adventist facility we rented in downtown San Jose, California. I was about a fourth of the way through a message on the prayer the Lord taught to His disciples when the Holy Spirit interrupted my lecture. My mind was suddenly occupied with one thought. It was almost as though I could hear him say: "This will not cause them to pray. Why don't you share the burden I've given you?"

Instantly, I was nearly overcome with passion. Words began to spill out of my mouth in a torrent as scripture after scripture was delivered word for word from Isaiah and Jeremiah, verses I had never memorized.

"I hate your new moon festivals and appointed feasts, they have become a burden to Me....you draw near with your lips, but your heart is far from Me. For My people have committed two evils: they have forsaken Me, the fountain of living waters, and hewn themselves cisterns—broken cisterns that can hold no water." And on and on! I had never spoken with such vehemence, yet felt no personal anger toward the people. Finally, the scripture found in Revelation 3:14–22: "Because you are neither hot nor cold, but lukewarm, I will spit you out of My mouth…He who has an ear, let him hear what the Spirit says to the churches."

With that last scripture I threw my Bible down on the pulpit, fell to my knees and began to sob uncontrollably. People began to weep and confess their sins. For two hours the deep conviction of the Spirit seemed to alternate with almost hilarious joy as many wept, laughed, or cried out to God. Later, as Rachel and I drove through the downtown streets on our way home, the common sight of a homeless person brought me to tears again. I was certain that this was the beginning of revival. At 35 years old I had witnessed some powerful works of the Spirit and had suffered little disillusionment; surely God was about to move in an extraordinary way!

An Invisible Barrier

Yet sadly, within a week, everything returned to normal. Though I now preached with greater zeal, boldness and freedom, the Word seemed to have little impact on most of the congregation. Though we shared the love of Christ from door to door and ministered to the homeless poor, the revival I prayed for every day never came.

Finally, we merged our fellowship with a larger congregation with which we had a long-standing relationship. We hoped that the strength springing from unity would surpass the combined results of our individual efforts. Soon after, Rachel and I were sent north to "plant" a church in the Sacramento area. We renewed our hopes that God would do a "new thing" in the new work we began. Yet scores of "break-out" meetings, powerful prophecies, prayer vigils, fasts, cairos moments, impartations, deliverances, evangelistic, apostolic, prophetic and pathetic conferences passed, and 10 years later I was still asking the same question: *Where are we missing it?*

I do not want to seem ungrateful for the many wonderful things that God has done in the past. Yes, I have seen lives transformed with miraculous healings and supernatural interventions. I have witnessed seemingly impossible doors opened and numerous prophetic revelations. Yet these have been mercy drops compared to the "normal" Christian life we read about in the scriptures. And something else became increasingly disturbing. Most of the people I considered to be in my care seemed to reach a certain level of maturity and then stop growing. I was convinced that God had equipped us with every tool necessary to grow a called individual from new convert to disciple-maker. But the frustrating reality was that even the most "advanced" leaders seemed to be crippled by a pattern of false starts, failure and ensuing guilt. I had taxed every resource within and without, striving through counseling, discipleship groups and prayer vigils to make sure we were rooted and grounded in love as well as in the Word. I had labored to enable each member to discover their gifting and to provide venues in which to practice them. Still, our dreams and goals remained unfulfilled. It seemed as though neither our best efforts nor even outpourings from above were able to break the invisible barrier keeping us from victory.

Disturbing Illusion

Equally unsettling was the illusion most of the congregation seemed to have about me. I did my best to adopt an equipping and coaching role, staying in the background until it was "preaching time," while encouraging them to step out in their gifts. I tried to be transparent from the pulpit and on a one-to-one basis. My goal was to see them excel in their "spiritual exploits" beyond anything I had achieved. Yet somehow they saw me as being categorically different than themselves. I was special, in a class by myself. I was to be treated differently, expected to know everything and was perceived as living a standard they felt they could never achieve. After all, I was *the Pastor*.

Disillusionment is a dirty word among those whose very self-worth is wrapped up in perceived success and the ability to display an optimistic attitude and shining example for all to follow. Yet I am convinced that the Holy Spirit revealed the sad truth that I was living an illusion.

I had labored under the illusion that we were a ministry founded and built on relationship. My preaching, discipleship and counseling emphasized intimacy with Christ and love for one another. I believed that out of that characteristic would flow the power of the Spirit, resulting in the realization of all that the church was to be. Yet I was blind to the obstacles that I, myself, had put in the way of pure relationship as Father had designed it to be.

Desperate for Change

This revelation sowed seeds of desperation deep within me. Undoubtedly, there had been seasons during which God had begun a cleansing work in my own life and had touched the congregation in a significant way. Yet it was clear that a radical transformation must take place, and I was unwilling to go on without it. But I was out of fresh ideas and wary of counsel that spoke contrary to my convictions. I was on the edge of a cliff with no place to go and without a trick left in my bag. Yet Father's purpose was to lead me and those I walk with on a challenging and exciting journey toward discovering a more excellent way. The following pages are intended to chronicle the portion of that journey that has been traveled at this writing. Perhaps some of the discoveries we have made along the way will bring new freedom to you as they have to me and others.

2

BACK TO THE FUTURE

*"Set you up highway markers..., make
yourself guideposts; turn your thoughts and
attention to the way by which you went [into
exile]; retrace your steps..."*
Selected from Jeremiah 31:21 (Amplified Version)

The static roar of the raging falls all but
drowned out my voice as I cried out to the Lord.
Embarrassed by my fear, I apologized for failing to
trust Him in this crisis. As the panic subsided, I
confessed my inability to make a decision: should
I attempt to negotiate the washout or turn back? I
felt prompted to turn back. After the decision was

made, peace erased most of the remaining fear, but I knew that one misstep could decide my fate.

The flip flops tended to hamper sure footing, so, beginning with my right foot, I pointed my toes toward the canyon floor hundreds of feet below and watched the flimsy footwear float gracefully through space until they disappeared. The heavy camera case full of equipment hanging from my neck interfered with delicate balance, so... WAIT A MINUTE! NOT SO FAST! My camera and equipment were among my most prized possessions. As we were living on a shoestring at the time, they would not be replaced anytime soon without a miracle. *This is ridiculous,* I thought, *I'm weighing my life against a bag full of inanimate objects!* I slipped the thick strap over my head and dangled the leather case over the edge of the abyss. My fingers refused to open. *There's got to be another way,* I thought as I studied the trail before me. Only a couple of steps would bring me to a steep descent with precarious footing. It would be too risky to attempt it with the heavy camera case as the downward movement presented a totally different dynamic than the climb. Then I noticed a small bush growing out of the edge of the trail just below. Squatting, I gingerly hooked the camera strap over a branch and carefully lowered myself a couple of feet down the steep descent where I found an exposed root offering a hand hold. Hanging tightly to the root with my left hand, I was able to reach the camera strap with my right and transfer it to another branch lower down.

Happily, I managed to proceed this way until the trail leveled off for a stretch. I breathed a sigh of relief, though I knew that the real challenge would come when reaching the nearly vertical embankment that I had encountered when first beginning the climb. *Would I be able to find any niches that could provide a foothold for my descending weight on the cliff side?* I hoped so.

* * *

The church had just concluded three months of meeting four times a week to seek the Lord for a greater understanding of His purposes for us as a body of believers. We had canceled all regularly scheduled meetings and programs except for Sunday morning service and "children's church" and a substance abuse recovery group. The purpose was to better focus on this single goal. Tuesday through Friday would find the lonely, the duty bound and those hungry for more of God gathering in the sanctuary to pray and wait on the Lord. From the onset, I had a strong sense that the people must be self-motivated in this pursuit. Finding a neutral place to sit, I would often study the ceiling and twiddle my thumbs until someone broke the silence with a song, a prayer or comment.

Letting Go

As the days and weeks went on, people grew more secure in each other's presence. Open confession and honest discussion opened the door for the Spirit to begin working in many of us in the areas of selfishness, impure motives and misplaced priorities. Some members of the worship team discovered that their expression of worship before the people belied the reality of their daily lives. Others realized that they were motivated more by the desire to perform than to glorify God. Subsequently, the team was reduced to three people. It became apparent that God was encouraging us to let go of everything in our personal and "ministry" life that did not express an overflow of our relationship with Him. As with my struggle on the cliff in deciding whether or not to let my camera and equipment go, we needed to allow God to reveal to us what was a valuable tool and what was old baggage. We felt that God was directing us to retrace the steps that brought us to this point of relative ineffectiveness and mark the path to help deter us from making the same wrong turns in the future. I was not yet fully aware of the ramifications this directive would have on my life and the fellowship I "served," yet I knew that "church as usual" was gone forever.

Eventually the elders and deacons resigned their positions. My associate, Nancy, and I wondered if we should temporarily resign our positions as well. However, we felt that someone should be responsible for major decisions with the assistance of a general "leadership team" comprised of those who had formerly been elders and deacons. We were unable to see how we could fulfill the task without the authority we saw as being vested in our positions. Also, we thought it unwise to rock the boat any further. God, however, continued to do so.

As mentioned earlier, we had kept the "children's church" and a recovery group going. The talented young couple directing the childrens ministry resigned due to changes in their work schedules and continuing education. The substance abuse group simply withered away until the directors showed up one evening to find no one in attendance. We got the hint. What we had not canceled, God brought to and end without our help.

Yet all during this time, there was a sense of anticipation that God was about to do something new and exciting. The expressions of repentance and recommitment to Christ together with the fresh experience of allowing the Holy Spirit to lead the gathering times prompted one young man to exclaim, "It's happening; this is revival!" My having taken a more neutral role in the meetings encouraged others to "step out" in their gifts and to initiate ministry rather than wait for a recognized "leader" to do so. Those who met together regularly began to feel like crusading comrades on a journey to the Promised Land. And we all were looking forward to a series of meetings with a missionary from Mexico whose ministry was distinguished by reports that the dead were raised on a regular basis. Never again, we decided, would we be content with anything less than revival.

Motive Check

Finally, the "waiting" time came to an end, the dead-raising missionary from Mexico had come and gone, and we were eager to see how God would use revived people and Holy Spirit fire to restore the ministries we had set aside. Instead, it became clear as we sought Him on this issue that we were not to resume even one program. It began to dawn on me then that Father was leading us through a twofold process. First, He was beginning to deal with wrong motives and misplaced priorities that blinded us to the true nature of His love. The following incident may help to illustrate:

"But worship is my life!" Gayle cried when she first realized that God was asking her to lay down her role on the worship team. "There's no other time when I sense the Spirit moving through me as mightily and sense the Lord's presence so intimately as when I'm playing my keyboard and singing in a public setting." Not more than one week later, Gayle shared her heart during a Sunday morning meeting. "I am so thankful for the Lord's faithfulness to me!" she said. "I thought God was taking away something I treasured to punish me. Now I realize that he was giving me a precious gift. He took something that I had scheduled into a time slot one day a week and turned it into an intimate relationship with Him all week long! And now my worship is no longer based on the approval or indifference of the crowd, but directed to the only One who is worthy. He always loves it, and so do I."

Her comments reminded me of Paul's words recorded in Galatians 1:10: "Am I now trying to win the approval of men or of God? Or am I trying to please men? If I were still trying to please men, I would not be a servant of Christ."

Burning the Chaff

Secondly, God was removing the "ministry" that we had built on a wrong foundation. As the fire of His love was purifying our hearts, what we had built with wood, hay and stubble was being burned to ashes.

It was evident that Father was taking us back down the path that had somehow led us away from His intended purpose. In the process of "retracing our steps" we were discovering pitfalls that had caused us to stumble blindly toward an unreachable goal on a path of our own making. But the lessons learned at every pitfall revisited became road markers imprinted on our hearts and minds for the journey ahead.

I met with the leadership team with the intention of preparing them for what would most likely lay ahead for a church with no programs and without a definitive vision for the future. We realized that we could expect attrition rather than growth. We would most likely be criticized for the "unwise" choices we were making. Perhaps my associate and I would have to find another way to make a living. And what might be the response of the patriarchal overseer of the network of churches for which I was in charge of world missions? He had sent me to Sacramento with a clearly defined vision and great expectations. I could only imagine his chagrin when he learned of the latest antics of the man he had referred to as one of his most true spiritual sons and closest confidants.

My Greatest Fear

Perhaps one of my greatest concerns was my dear wife of almost 30 years. Rachel is my closest friend and most fearless critic. Her practical response to almost anything that comes her way contrasts with an oftentimes radically creative, and prophetic side that can impact the direction or intensity of any gathering. Rachel is always giving her hands-on best to every project and spending herself serving whoever has a need. Yet now she was insecure with the uncertainty of almost everything surrounding her life. My greatest fear lay in what my obedience might cost her. One of her greatest joys is giving. It seems that most days find her bright with anticipation as she wraps a gift to surprise someone with. Would I be able to support her generosity in the future?

It was clear that we were on an uncertain and perhaps dangerous path. Yet all agreed that there was no other acceptable alternative. We could only put our future as a church family in the hands of the only One who could lead us and keep us.

* * *

I was sitting in my favorite prayer chair in my office one afternoon pouring my heart out to God when the intercom buzzed. Noticing the blinking "hold" light I was about to ask the secretary to take a message when I felt checked by the Holy Spirit. *This is not an interruption, it's an answer.*

As I reached for the phone, I could hardly wait to see what the answer would be. Placing the receiver to my ear I heard the voice of an acquaintance from whom I had not heard in over a year. "Would you mind if I brought a book by your office?"

"Of course not," I answered. I was looking forward to seeing Jim again. I had first met him at a monthly gathering of pastors from around the greater

Sacramento area that I had initiated and facilitated for several years. The last time I saw him, we had met over lunch where we had shared our mutual longing to see the church return to its roots.

As Jim walked into my office and began to share, his eyes seemed to glow with fresh enthusiasm and renewed purpose. Soon he handed me a small book that told the story of a church in an eastern state from which he had just returned. "You wouldn't believe what I experienced there," he said. "The people were like one happy family and every meal time was like Thanksgiving Day! There were no regularly scheduled meetings," he went on excitedly, "yet everything flowed like clockwork. I witnessed spontaneous healings that took place during worship. The people operate in a true spirit of community, loving freely and generously meeting one another's needs."

After Jim left, I grabbed the little book and began reading hungrily. The first few pages were a diary recording eight normal days in the life of the ministry Jim had described. As I continued to read, I began to weep. This was what my weary heart had been yearning for. The words my hungry eyes were devouring could have been an account from the book of Acts. They also reminded me of the beginnings of a ministry that I had been a part of for 15 years before being sent to Sacramento.

Blast From the Past

It was in the mid '70s when the "Jesus movement" days were winding down and the charismatic movement was heating up. A middle-aged widow named Pat Severson found herself in a meeting hall full of teenagers from every walk of life. She had been youth director for the Northern California and Nevada areas of the denomination she represented. Yet the church she served in San Jose dismissed her when she brought in so many young people that the leadership feared for the welfare of the facilities' new carpets! Needing help ministering to the many needy youth, Pat gathered some people together for prayer and ended up with an enthusiastic and adventurous team from varied backgrounds. Gary worked for an "underground" rock station and sported an afro hairdo. He met Christ after overdosing on drugs and now had an unquenchable appetite for the things of God. Rod was from a Lutheran background, worked in a bank, was in love with everyone and had a golden voice. Richard met Christ during the Jesus movement. He had combed the beaches of Southern California sharing Christ with everyone he met. Leona had been Pat's prayer partner for many years and had a background with Christian Missionary Alliance. Rachel came from an Assembly of God background and I was raised with a Conservative Baptist influence. She was working as a waitress and I was a landscape construction estimator.

We began inviting youth to our homes for "Jesus raps" and soon were meeting in 14 different houses around town. Although most of the young people claimed to be agnostic or even atheistic, their hunger for God was obvious. Soon we were baptizing converts in swimming pools and rejoicing as we watched God transform lives. Once when a couple of us went to visit a young lady in the hospital, Rod took his guitar and began to play and sing worship songs beside her bed. Soon a couple of ambulatory patients were standing at the door of her room listening in. It wasn't long before the nurses were asking us to visit various patients in the ward. Within weeks we were ministering in hospitals on a regular basis. In the same way, God opened the door to prisons, juvenile detention facilities, halfway houses, rest homes, and psychiatric facilities. But the hallmark of the group that we called Mobile Ministries was the love and acceptance that flowed among us and out to the people we touched.

Love God and Love the People

"We've been given only two instructions," Pat used to say, "love God and love the people." There was only one other rule: "Do whatever He tells you to do." The motto for ministry: "Love them like they are, and tell it like it is."

Armed with these simple instructions, we discovered the joy of touching others with Father's love and the thrill of following the Spirit. We also witnessed the power of God.

"Wait, wait!" cried an excited voice as we moved down a hospital corridor. We turned around just as a middle aged lady caught up with us, her eyes filled with amazement. In the moments before, our little team had held hands in the elevator, forgiving and loving one another after there had been a misunderstanding between a couple members of the team that were ministering at Santa Clara Hospital that evening. The love was sweet once again as we moved toward the nurses station. "You won't believe what just happened," the lady said incredulously. "My leg was injured and I could hardly walk, but when you all passed by me, I was healed!"

We saw a genuine move of God take place in the juvenile hall and rejoiced to see troubled youth transformed. Some of us even had the privilege of watching deaf and dumb people speak. Finally, we "planted" a church in downtown San Jose.

But as we became more organized and less spontaneous, the power of the Spirit became less evident, and the fresh excitement of the early days began to fade away. Now that we had learned how to "do it," the child-like wonder and dependence on the Holy Spirit was replaced with calculated anticipation and preplanned strategy. Moreover, now that we were more "mature" and had assumed various positions in ministry, expectations were placed upon one another. Consequently, relationships became strained. Eventually the merger mentioned in Chapter 1 took place. Thus began a decade during which I continually strived unsuccessfully to recapture the essence of what I had once known.

Now, as I continued to read the little book that stirred up such poignant memories, I recalled how often during the past 10 years I had sensed the nudge of the Holy Spirit urging me not to forget what we had learned in the early days of Mobile Ministries. God was moving in our hearts to draw us back to our first Love.

Return to Basics

I realized that we must simply return to loving God and loving the people He placed in our path. I sensed that this "blast from the past" could be speaking volumes about our future. Several prophecies given to me during that time had also pointed to a change that God wanted to bring to our fellowship. Finally my eyes were beginning to open, and I felt like a one week old kitten surveying the world around me for the first time. The words before me provided a biblical foundation for the truth that had already begun to ring in my heart. Church as I had understood it was about to be redefined. I knew that I must research the scriptures with a wide open heart and a fresh set of lenses.

Though I was encouraged and fascinated by the account of church life in the little book I was reading, I understood that it might look completely different for us. Part of what makes life with Father such an adventure is that He never seems to do the same thing the same way twice. My desire was to let go of everything else and take Father's hand so that He could lead me step by step.

3

ONE CHIEF EXTRA

"God is going to release to you a new revelation, an illumination, some new ways involving leadership and church structure... Do not get caught in any ruts; do not pattern after others. I will put a new vision in your heart and you are going to do a new thing, and you're going to do it My way. You can't wait for the agreement of all others, even some you fellowship with now. They will try to get you to compromise... Write it on stone tablets."

(Prophetic word to author from Leon Walters in 1991—nine years prior to beginning the "journey.")

Riding high on the encouragement garnered from the little book and the memory lesson from Mobile Ministries, I was now confident regarding how God was leading us and in what general direction we were to go. On the other hand, I was clueless as to how to proceed. To complicate matters, the decisions we had made to cancel programs put a strain on our relationship with the leader of the network with whom we were associated. Furthermore, we were growing in a fresh understanding regarding leadership that stood in stark contrast to his beliefs on the subject. It was painful for me to disappoint this fatherly man of God whose friendship I held dear and whose life and ministry I so greatly admired. Yet unmistakably, God was leading us on a path that forced us to make a decision. As a leader in the network, I could not dishonor my elder by encouraging principles that contradicted his convictions. Clearly, a confrontation was imminent.

A Critical Decision

As I began to speculate on the ramifications that we might face at this juncture, it appeared that the "retracing of our steps" could be far more harrowing than the path we had negotiated thus far. Can one become disengaged from a 14 year ministry connection and leadership position without threatening the personal relationship with disaster?

Without question, it should be not merely possible, but expected. Still, understanding that relationship and ministry partnership seemed woven into an almost inseparable strand that defined this particular ministry. I feared the worst.

My mom had come out from Colorado to California for our daughter's wedding and accepted our invitation to stay on with Rachel and me for a month. Her husband, (my step father) had passed away six months earlier, so she was considering our offer to move in with us permanently.

It was a Sunday afternoon, and the three of us were enjoying casual conversation over fried chicken at the local Colonel Sanders. "I noticed you didn't take an offering for that network pastor as (our network leader) requested," Rachel commented.

"I didn't feel right about it," I replied. "When I checked with Nancy (my associate) she felt the same way."

Rachel reached for a biscuit and broke off a bite sized piece. "It's time to end our commitment to the network." She spoke with the settled conviction that was always evident when she was aware that the Holy Spirit was confirming her thoughts. I stopped munching on my chicken leg for a moment, not sure of the direction she was heading. Was this the same lady who felt so secure under the "covering" of someone older and wiser? Was this my wife speaking who believed it was vital that we were connected with something bigger than ourselves? I resumed chewing slowly as Rachel continued. "As long as we remain under (the network leader's) authority, we are obligated to support his goals and the goals of the network we serve. On the other hand, God cannot bless us in the new understanding He has given us until we sever our alignment with the old."

Rachel's words struck a chord within me that seemed to resonate through my entire being. Suddenly I was reminded of several pivotal moments in my life where Father had called my attention to His absolute sovereignty over my gifts and calling. As I began to share with these two special women in my life, my heart seemed to swell with a sense of Father's love and nearness. The first related incident that came to mind took place in 1987.

I had just finished teaching a class at a bible school in Waipahu, Hawaii. "Tell me about your father." Jake, the school's director, took me by surprise with his question as I had not mentioned my father nor made reference to myself or family during the session. We were about to place our lunch orders at a fast food joint specializing in Hawaiian hamburgers and Huli Huli chicken. I turned to glance at the man standing beside me and paused while I considered how to answer him. Meanwhile, my thoughts entertained early childhood memories.

My father remained single until he was 45. Then he met my mother at New Tribes Missions training center in Northern California. While on their first mission trip to Xuaxaca, Mexico, my mother became pregnant with Carl before the couple returned to settle near Nogales, Arizona just south of the Mexican border. There they joined two other missionary families to form a small community they named Bethel Acres. My father built our house from the ground up and kept the vehicles running. He made slingshots, drew cartoons and taught us how to shoot a gun. We raised goats and chickens and alfalfa hay and rode an old mare named Silver Bell.

People, Prayer and Passion

From there the men of Bethel Acres traveled into Mexico and preached a message of grace to those whose spiritual eyes were blinded by good-works-based religion and superstition. They returned with tales of encounters with demonized wild men intent on their destruction and scores of newly-unbound souls weeping for joy at their new-found freedom in Christ. When I became old enough to understand, I sat spellbound as they recounted their adventures and was moved by my father's passion for souls. But there was one thing about my dad that created a desire deep within me that remains to this day. Not 500 yards from our house was a forest where some of the largest mesquite trees in the world grew. Normally the size of a small bush, many of these mesquites grew as tall as oak trees and densely populated about 30 acres. In a small clearing in the middle of these woods was my father's "prayer log." Sometimes I met him hours after he had disappeared into the woods as he returned with tear stained cheeks and eyes bright with child-like wonder and delight. He would take my hand and we would stroll for the rest of the way home singing joyful songs of faith.

After we placed our order, I shared a few memories of my dad with Jake.

"You picked up his mantle, didn't you?" he offered. The thought had never crossed my mind. I had always thought of Pat Severson as my "spiritual father." It was her life and teaching that helped school me in the things of the Spirit and the work of the ministry. Yet something about Jake's words rang true deep within me. Suddenly I recalled the strange declaration Pat had made to me as she joined me at the altar that memorable Sunday morning recounted in Chapter One. "That did not come from what I've taught you" she said, referring to the explosive torrent of words that had poured out of my soul. I waited for an explanation, but none was forthcoming. Yet clearly she was impacted by what had happened and understood her statement to be significant.

A Defining Moment

As I pondered Jake's comment it became clear what God wanted me to understand: my natural father was my spiritual father as well. But why was that so important? I was grateful for the godly heritage passed down from my father as well as from my saintly mother whose life has always exemplified joyous servanthood and whose tireless labors in prayer still uphold all those she loves. But my father had passed away 14 years earlier. It was true that my relationship with Pat seemed to be changing. As her health began to deteriorate, the responsibility for the expanding ministry fell more heavily upon me. Perhaps God was preparing me for her retirement. But what did that have to do with my father?

* * *

As I came to this part of the story at Colonel Sanders that day, the truth could not have come to me more clearly or with greater intensity than if God had spoken to me in an audible voice. *I called you from your birth. You belong to me, not to man. It was I who placed a mandate on your life, and no man can change it. You must decide whether you are going to submit to me or to man.* When I spoke out the words that were burning in my mind and spirit the presence of the Lord was overwhelming and tears began to blur my

41

vision. My earthly "spiritual father" was dead. He had cultivated my desire to know God and to follow Him. Others had spoken into my life and helped to equip me for works of service. But God alone was my true spiritual Father, and it was to Him only that I owed my allegiance and loving obedience. I left the restaurant knowing that I must contact the network overseer as soon as possible. Although dreading the confrontation that seemed unavoidable, I was filled with a sense of peace and liberty of spirit.

Confrontation

The meetings with the network leader were as painful to Rachel and me as I had anticipated. I tried to explain that my respect and attitude toward him had not changed in the least, yet I could not dishonor him by teaching and leading in a way that contradicted his own convictions and directives. Yet he was unwilling to honor a relationship that did not include organizational commitment and submission to his authority. He said that I was rebellious and deceived. After two meetings and eight hours of intense debate had failed to change either of our convictions, we hugged and he prayed for me before we parted ways.

Rachel and I were numb in the wake of a 15 year relationship ending in such a traumatic fashion. I grieved for the pain that I was causing to a man whom I loved and respected. Still, I felt that a huge weight had been lifted from me. I realized that for the first time I felt free to do whatever I believed God was leading me to do.

Yet there was another reality uncovered by this excruciating ordeal and the self examination that ensued. What effect had my style of leadership imposed on those I had viewed as under my care?

Truthquake!

I found Bob H. at the salad bar in the pizza joint where we had agreed to meet, loading up his plate with every conceivable item. Tall, slender and balding early, Bob has a voracious appetite and an intense personality. He had served me faithfully for 18 years, leaving his job and moving his family when we left San Jose to begin the work in Sacramento. We had shared our dreams, victories and failures, laughed and cried together, prayed together and walked together through some deep waters. Yet today as we carried our pizza, salad and drinks to the table I was uncertain of what our lunch meeting would reveal.

Almost a year earlier we had discarded positions and titles. We had set the people free from assigned duties to pursue a relationship with the Lord that we hoped would be unencumbered by any motives other than love (more about that later). Ever since those changes were made, Bob had grown increasingly distant. Now, as my glance engaged his piercing blue eyes across the table, I asked him what had happened to our relationship. I was startled by Bob's answer.

"I don't feel like I have a relationship with you anymore," he said. Bob reached for a slice of garlic chicken pizza while mine stuck in my throat. "My relationship with you has always been based on your position as senior pastor and my role in serving you," he said. "Somehow I found my purpose and identity in relating to you on that basis." A hint of anger brought a slight edge to his voice. "Now, with all the rules changed, I no longer know who I am. Who I am has always been wrapped up in what I do," he continued, "and in my service to you as the senior pastor. Now that I'm no longer under you, or serving your vision, I have none of my own. In fact," he went on, "I don't think I have a relationship with the Lord. With no one to perform for, I'm totally lost. I don't know how to relate to God *or* you anymore."

Reality Check

The conversation with Bob and many others stingingly brought harsh reality into sharp focus. If my long-time friend, co-laborer and confidant had based his very identity and relationship with Father on his performance, then we had missed one of the primary truths upon which Christ was

44

to build His church! How often had I preached with great passion that Christ had completed the work for us at the cross, and that our part was to identify with Him in His death and resurrection! I stressed that we need only to trust Him to complete in us what He had begun as we look to Him only and lean on Him wholly.

Yet we seemed motivated to perform by our need for acceptance or by the shame we felt when we neglected our duty or failed to meet the perceived expectations. As I was being "raised up" in the ministry, I was always taught that "the buck stops" at the senior pastor. When I failed to see the results that spelled success to me and to those whose authority I was "under," I felt as though I had let every one down. In turn, those who worked "under" me sensed my disappointment and became frustrated in their inability to please me. The result was that our relationship to God and to one another was tied to expectations we could never meet. I had often taught that we should be "rooted and grounded in love." I preached that this love was based on the unfathomable love of the Father, demonstrated through the cross of Christ who finished the work for us. Yet, somehow, my life and the way I led had modeled something far different.

A Stunning Revelation

As I continued to re-examine familiar scriptures regarding leadership and authority, I became convinced that much of what I had believed and practiced was in absolute contradiction to the word of God. Jesus clearly warned His disciples against adopting the hierarchical form of leadership that ruled the Gentile world in their day as well the positional model that marked the Jewish religious world.*

*Matthew 20:25–28(NASB) "...You know that the rulers of the Gentiles lord it over them, and their great men exercise authority over them. IT IS NOT SO AMONG YOU, but whoever wishes to become great among you must be your servant, and whoever wishes to be first among you must be your slave; just as the Son of Man did not come to be served, but to serve, and to give His life a ransom for many." (See also Luke 22:25–26) It seems clear that these passages reveal that Jesus is not simply decrying overbearing leaders as such, but the hierarchical form of leadership based on the concept that authority flows from the top down. Unfortunately, this "chain of command" style of leadership, common to the world system, is often adopted by the church system of today. Matthew 23:8–12(NASB) "...But do not be called Rabbi; for One is your Teacher, and you are all brothers. And do not call anyone on earth your father; for One is your Father, He who is in heaven. And do not be called leaders; for One is your leader, that is, Christ. But the greatest among you shall be your servant. And whosoever exalts himself shall be humbled; and whoever humbles himself shall be exalted." It is of note that nowhere in the epistles are spiritual leaders addressed by a title. When Paul refers to himself as "Paul an apostle," he is stating his call to function in a particular gifting, but never do we read of anyone referring to "apostle Paul" or "Pastor Epaphroditus."

Jesus explained that those worldly forms of leadership contrasted sharply with the kingdom model of sacrificial servanthood and child-like humility. They were not to have honorific titles that set them apart from the brotherhood as a specialist in the Body of Christ. Rather, they were to be those who washed the feet of others, thereby taking the position of a slave.

Positional Authority or Abuse?

As I pondered Bob's identity crisis, I realized that I had unwittingly usurped the place of Christ in his life by assuming a position that belonged to Him alone! I failed to understand that any authority operating in my life was functional only as I acted in response to Christ; I held no "office" or static position* inherent of authority.

*It is important to note that nowhere in New Testament ecclesiastical vocabulary do we find the words "office" or "position" used in the original language. *Diakonia* (meaning service) and *praxis* (meaning doing, practice, function) are mistranslated as "office" in some versions of the Bible. The conspicuous absence of words in the Greek denoting rank and file leadership, inherent power, ruler or chief corresponds with the fact that leadership as notated in the New Testament is described functionally and authority operates organically through the life flowing from God by His Spirit. The power and authority to *do* always came from *being* (of godly character, maturity, humility), never from the inherent power of a static office or position. In contrast to spiritual authority, Romans 13 discusses the relationship of the believer to civil servants who rule by virtue of the official position they hold. In such regard, submission is rightly due the official, irrespective of his character or other personal virtues. Thus, if a corrupt police officer is enforcing a given law, one must obey him in deference to the uniform he is wearing. His uniform identifies his position of authority; his character or worthiness to hold such a position is an altogether separate issue. It is most unfortunate that official or positional authority is often applied to church structure, for it lends an unwarranted and potentially dangerous power to control to an elite few while excluding those without an official position from contributing in areas where they may be most gifted.

Furthermore, in my efforts to fulfill the "position" of "Senior Pastor", (a role completely unsupported in scripture), I had assumed an area and measure of responsibility that made my place in the body uniquely indispensable. The effect was that Bob viewed me as an earthly representation of God's authority, even representing Christ in that respect. Thus, serving me was serving Christ; adopting my vision and helping me to fulfill it was his mission, believing as I believed was important towards maintaining unity. The result was that Bob's relationship with Father God was being mediated through me! Remove the middle-man (title and position) and Bob's sense of identity was lost. And because he felt he must please me in order to please God, he no longer knew how to evaluate his relationship with Father.

Bob's response to the hierarchical/positional form of leadership commonly modeled in the religious institutions today may seem extreme to many reading these pages. Or the reader may deduce from this example that we were excessive in our use of authority. However, in interviews with believers from widely varied "church" backgrounds, I have heard the same theme repeated in many ways. Truth be told, authority exercised to any degree in the wrong context is for that very reason excessive and even abusive.

Saved by Grace

As these truths slowly penetrated my understanding, I was struck with a painful reality. Every individual in the group I had led up to the present, as well as all those who had parted ways with us in the past, must be affected to varying degrees by what I now held to be unscriptural leadership structure and practice.

Yet, though some were undergoing an identity crisis similar to what Bob was experiencing, others were enjoying new found freedom in their relationship with God and with one another. They were being delivered *from* confusion regarding their identity.

"I feel like I've been born again, *again!*" Lynn cried in one of the gatherings. "For the first time in my life, I'm becoming free from the bondage to my family's acceptance of me. I don't have to judge my self-worth by who I was or by what I can do, but only by the fact that God really loves *me*...I'm beautiful in Him!"

Soon Bob would find a fresh identity and new beginning in his relationship with Father as well. Yet I grieved over the fact that much of the healing going on in the body would never have been necessary if I had taken my hands off of God's church long ago. What a blessing it was to remember that His forgiveness is free, His love is unfailing and His redemption is complete! Moreover, God is so much bigger than either my mistakes or my successes! I am convinced that the working of His love and grace in each of the lives adversely affected will be so much the greater for the loss they have suffered. Still, my failures are a constant reminder to be very careful with the fragile treasures that God gives us in one another.

4

LET MY PEOPLE GO!

"For this reason I kneel before the Father, from whom his whole family in heaven and earth derives it's name. –But you are a chosen people, a royal priesthood, a holy nation, a people belonging to God..."

(Eph 3:14a–15, 1Pet.2:9a)

"How is *your* church doing?"

"*My* people never remember what last week's sermon was about."

Have you ever heard a couple of "pastors" discussing "church" with one another? Given the possessive nouns scattered throughout the conversation, you would think they were chatting about their respective privately owned businesses. I must confess that I was guilty of the same. Of course I knew that the people belonged to God. But as I saw myself to be the principle under-shepherd that Christ had appointed to build this particular expression of His church, the perceived successes and failures involved became my personal victories or defeats. I believed that I either had to have all the answers or the ability to find them. Certainly God wouldn't have put me in this capacity unless He had equipped me with spiritual eyes and ears that were just a bit sharper than the most mature saint in the fellowship. And since it was I to whom He gave the vision I would most naturally be the one who knew best how to get there!

But as my concept of "Senior Pastor" crumbled under the re-examination of the word and subsequent revelation born out of disturbing experiences with real people, I knew that I had become a bottleneck to the forward movement of God's people. As a modified priest, I had blocked the release of the royal priesthood!

Mediated Christianity

"There's a couple outside that need some money for gas." Bob Schneider was leaning over my shoulder just before an interactive Sunday morning Bible study was about to begin. I glanced up at him and waited. Burly and with both arms sporting lavish tattoos, Bob was street-wise and compassionate. "I think these folks are for real; I don't sense a con job here," he said. I smiled and shrugged. "Well, you're the pastor; he said, "tell me what to do!" I shook my head in amazement. It had been months since I had discarded that title. There had been many open discussions and teaching on our new understanding of leadership, and I had quit telling people what to do long ago. "What do *you* think we should do?" I asked. Bob answered quickly; "I think we should ask the group for a donation of loose change and send the folks on their way." "Great," I answered, "do what you think is right." Bob took up a collection and blessed the couple who ended up returning for the larger gathering.

The above incident serves to illustrate several of the effects of unscriptural leadership upon those who are being led. Perhaps the most significant offence touches the ability and privilege of an individual to hear God for themselves. Bob had both the background and gifting to help him accurately discern the will of God regarding the need at hand. I, on the other hand, did not. What discernment I may have had in the past regarding the needy had become dull after seemingly 99% of the considerable number of those asking for assistance throughout the years turned out to be practiced "workers of the system." Yet, in the past, without my confirmation, Bob would have questioned his discernment. In short, he would have depended on me to hear God for him. Such mediated Christianity challenges one's access to Father and their growth of intimacy with Him. I am not questioning the wisdom of soliciting the confirmation of others when we are seeking the direction of the Lord in important matters. In question here is the misconception that a leader as such is better qualified to determine the will of God than one not so recognized.

Misused Authority

Secondly, for one person to retain the authority to grant permission for another to move on what he feels is right is to negate the individual believer's authority in Christ. Bob wanted me to tell him what to do so that:

1. he would not have to risk my disapproval should he move contrary to my desires, and:

2. he would save himself the burden of responsibility. God lamented through the prophet, Jeremiah, that *the priests rule by their own authority, and my*

people love it this way (Jer. 5:31).
If I don't trust others to make the right
decisions, I will take the responsibility on
personally to spare myself the risk of failure
and, perhaps, to avoid being found a poor
steward of "the ministry." Ironically, the
opposite is true. By not releasing others to
exercise their gifts freely, I will ultimately be
crushed by undue responsibility and prove to
be a poor steward of God's resources as well.

3. If we only allow people to operate in their
gifts in a controlled environment such as
designated meetings, etc., their freedom to
mature is hindered and their relationship to
the body in that capacity will be artificial.

Bob had been an exceptional participant in
the discipleship group that served as our primary
leadership training tool for a year. We studied and
memorized scripture together, assigned outreach
during the week, participated in work days, and
set standards for righteous living. Every three
"disciples" were assigned to a designated "leader"
who was available to them during the week. But
the highlight of the weekly agenda was the Sunday
evening service. This was "run" exclusively by the
discipleship group and was the venue in which
they practiced preaching, teaching, worship
leading, "body ministry", etc. The meeting became
so popular that it was at times as well attended as
Sunday morning.

Misplaced Dependency

Every program we initiated was designed to help participants to grow in godly character, develop their gifts and to learn to walk in the Spirit. Yet, as mentioned in the first chapter, something seemed to block the continuation of spiritual growth and maturity. I now understand that people were not fully free to grow in their relationship with Christ in the context of the body according to the uniquely personal way that God had designed just for them. Rather, they measured their spiritual walk against the expectations (whether perceived or real) of the leadership, especially the "senior pastor." Wayne Jacobsen states in the December 2002 issue of *Body Life* found on his website, lifestream.org, that "the perception of church...is so dependant on the leadership of men and women that many cannot imagine how to function without it. That is tragic, because if our dependency isn't in Christ, we will never discover the power and simplicity of body life."

Furthermore, if one feels affirmed by "the pastor," he is satisfied, if he does not feel affirmed by the pastor, neither will he recognize affirmation from God. In short, the pastor has, in the lives of many, become a spiritual guru who has an exclusive hotline to God. He may be a humble, unassuming individual with a servant's heart and an aversion to controlling anyone. Yet the very nature of positional authority wrapped in the honorific title that comes with the package separates him from the rest of the folks who often see him as a professional holy man.

I will never forget the comment of one lady who was giddy to be in the home of the well known pastor of a large fellowship she attended. At one point he left the room and was absent for several minutes. The guest turned to the pastor's wife and asked where he might be. "I think that he is using the restroom," she replied. The woman's eyes grew wide with astonishment. Putting her hand to her mouth, she drew in her breath: "I never thought of pastor as having to use the toilet!"

The incident, though astounding, is not uniquely outlandish. Incredibly, I have, on several occasions, been told by mentally competent individuals that they thought I was perfect until they saw me make a mistake! This was offered without embarrassment on the individual's part although I had often shared my shortcomings from the pulpit when these individuals were in attendance.

Exalted by Title

These stories may be amusing, but they highlight the tragic phenomena that occur when a brother or sister is exalted above the rest of the royal priests by a position and title.

And somehow, that false place of honor causes the untitled to feel less than royal priests themselves. For the moment one receives another person as an earthly representative of Christ, he will lose sight of the heavenly reality. He will assume that he will never be able to reach the level of spirituality that seems to belong to "The Man (or Woman) of God." Consequently, he becomes content to remain a passenger to be pulled along in the wake of his spiritual hero.

Others fare quite differently. They are the ones whose leadership gifts have been recognized by those "in charge" and are given special attention and training. They are excited by the chance to "move up the ladder" and work hard toward that goal. If they please the powers that be, they may become a full time minister! Every pat on the back from the Big Man causes their heart to swell with pride; any sign of displeasure can fill them with anxiety. Not to say that their motives are always impure. Most often, a true love for God and His Word initiate their desire to be equipped. Still, the rules of the system dictate an expected response that can redirect focus and drive. And when we depend on man for our sense of worth and/or well-being, we leave ourselves wide open to an abusive relationship.

Flying home from China after a "scouting" trip, I glanced over at John, (not his real name), a gifted young man whom I was "grooming" to one day replace me as senior pastor. His eyes were alive with the thoughts and questions filling his brain. Finally, he cleared his throat and asked, "How would you evaluate this trip on a scale of one to ten?"

"I would give it about an eight," I replied. "We were able to hike into a remote area and touch an un-reached people group. We met some key contacts working near the Burmese border, and we learned much about potential ministry in the future. All in all, I feel it was a successful mission." John's eyes smiled with satisfaction. Then he broached the subject that I was hoping not to address until after the excitement of his first mission's trip had cooled. "How would you grade our performance as a team?"

Spiritual Manipulation

Our team had included one of John's co-workers and a veteran missionary to China who had hosted us for the duration of the visit. True to his training as a former Navy Seal, John had taken charge in practical issues and covered his own bases, expecting each of us to do likewise. I had been particularly annoyed when, during a torrential downpour in Li Jong, he set off at such a pace that we became separated. We had no rendezvous point, and I was left to wander until I stumbled onto the group shortly afterwards. I was used to being served and looked out for by those aspiring to be leaders. John's mode of operation struck me as independent and inconsiderate. (I suspect now that God identified *my* mode of operation as that of a pompous jackass, and decided that I should trot around in the rain until my jets were cooled.) At any rate, several other small issues had annoyed me as well, and as we talked on the way home, I broke these things to John as gently as I could. I was startled to see his blue eyes fill with tears. The rest of the flight home was quiet and a bit strained. Months later when John and his family "moved on" he indicated our "awkward relationship" as being a primary contributing factor to their decision.

At the time, I judged that John was too sensitive to be able to receive correction as one who wanted to be trained. How, I wondered, did he survive as a Navy Seal? Yet, looking back, I realize that criticism from me had much greater implications in his mind due to the power of my "position." Added to that fact was his longing for a father figure to help fill the gap that was left by his natural father from whom John had been separated for many years since just before entering his teens. Yes, John was definitely tough enough to brave the rigorous and even brutal training that eliminates all but the strongest and most persevering of those with enough guts to try out for the special forces. But no one is built to withstand the emotional abuse that results when spiritual life is manipulated by a worldly leadership structure and philosophy masquerading as kingdom authority.

Free to Live a Free Life

It is the Father's desire that His children serve Him from a single motive: that of pure and simple devotion to Christ. Yet many of us serve a system that is designed to motivate people by exploiting their need for approval and affirmation. Equally damaging to our relationship with Father is the sense of duty imposed upon us by a structure that requires our "faithful participation" to sustain its momentum. When we find ourselves lacking the desire to serve or attend whatever may be encouraged by leadership, we may be prodded into compliance by a sense of guilt or shame. Pleasing men, a competitive spirit, guilt and shame: these are the very bondages that Christ died to deliver us from.

These enemies of the soul rob us of the freedom and joy which characterizes the love relationship with the Father that each of us was born to enjoy. I like the way The Message translation phrases Galatians 5:1–6.

Christ has set us free to live a free life. So take your stand! Never let anyone put a harness of slavery on you.

I am emphatic about this. The moment any one of you submits to circumcision or any other rule-keeping system, at that same moment Christ's hard-won gift of freedom is squandered. I repeat my warning: The person who accepts the ways of circumcision trades all the advantages of the free life in Christ for the obligations of the slave life of the law. I suspect you would never intend this, but this is what happens. When you attempt to live by your own religious plans and projects, you are cut off from Christ; you fall out of grace. Meanwhile we expectantly wait for a satisfying relationship with the Spirit. For in Christ, neither our most conscientious religion nor disregard of religion amounts to anything. What matters is something far more interior: faith expressed in love.

If I have been harsh in my assessments, it is the system I mean to condemn, not the people within it. I was as sincere as I knew how to be from the time that I "entered the ministry" until the day God mercifully began to open my eyes to see from a different perspective. Today I have many dear friends among those who still practice leadership the way I used to. These men are humble and have a sincere desire to see the body of Christ thrive and come to maturity, and they have my respect and admiration.

But I am convinced that the leadership structures supported by most of the religious institutions today have unwittingly robbed God's people of their privileges as royal priests. They have made them dependant upon mere men and upon a worldly system that shames them into allegiance while blinding them to the authority and freedom that is rightfully theirs in Christ. I believe that God is jealous for His people and longs for them to bask in the unfathomable depths of

His love. He yearns for them to know the freedom and inexpressible joy that comes from trustfully depending and leaning on Him only. And to all of us who help to care for His children, God is saying:,"Let my people go!"

5

FOLLOW THE LEADER

For it seems to me that God has put us on display at the end of the procession, like men condemned to die in the arena. We are fools for Christ... we are weak... we are dishonored. But we have this treasure in jars of clay to show that this all surpassing power is from God and not from us.

(Portions of 1Cor. 4:9,10, 2Cor. 4:7 NIV)

The large auditorium was filled with people. Tastefully decorated with carefully placed greenery, the expansive platform was brightly lit. I waited nervously behind the edge of the curtain just offstage. The air was electric with a sense of anticipation. Suddenly, I knew the moment had arrived. With a deadening sense of resignation I walked slowly, deliberately toward the exact center of the stage. There, a small, white toilet waited to receive me. After finishing my business, I awoke from the dream; then closed my eyes again in relief.

To many the word "leadership" evokes images of a dynamic individual with a charismatic personality. He or she is standing head and shoulders above the crowd commanding their rapt attention and solicitous response. This description may fit King Saul, but is hardly the picture painted for us of Jesus in either the Old or New Testaments. We see Him described as "having no form or comeliness that we should desire Him; a root growing out of dry ground." He is exposed before His people, mangled and bloody, almost naked, apparently defeated and un-esteemed. And in the midst of excruciating physical pain coupled with overwhelming mental and emotional anguish, He lovingly watched over His flock.

"Woman, behold your son!" Then He said to John, "Behold your mother!"

This passionate, yet tender utterance revealed the heart of the Shepherd who, in the very act of laying down His life for His friends reached out one last time in His final hour of anguish to provide for the lonely. In demonstrating the greatest act of love the world has ever known, Jesus revealed the nature of godly leadership. In meekly enduring the jeering insults and physical torture of His tormentors, Jesus gave us a glimpse into the depth of humility that characterized a life lived out in eager submission to the Father. Jesus made no effort to protect His image, to look good in the eyes of man. He was concerned only that His words and actions would be pleasing to His Father. And as He hung exposed before the world, He was not self-conscious; instead His concern was toward His friends and those who would one day come to know Him.

Transparent Living

Much has been said and written on the subject of humility, but I believe there is one aspect of its nature that is often overlooked, particularly by those who aspire to leadership. Some Bible colleges actually teach that a leader must keep from allowing the "members of his flock" to become too familiar with him. He must maintain a good image and demonstrate strong leadership at all times. I believe that Jesus showed the very opposite to be true. He invited His followers to live with Him, and to be with Him in His hour of weakness. They saw His heart break as He wept over Jerusalem and witnessed His exasperation with their slowness to understand. They watched His anger rise to the boiling point as He overturned tables and drove the money-changers out of the temple. He called them friends, and intimated that friends had nothing to hide.

It would stand to reason in light of the foregoing statements that one can lead only to the degree that he or she has established true relationships with those he or she has been called to touch for a season. And as friends, one of the most effective ways to help one another to grow in Christ is to walk together in our weaknesses and failures as well as our victories. It is true that Jesus never fell to sin or temptation. But His transparent lifestyle gives us a view of His relationship with Father as well as how He handled the many challenges to His humanness. Sometimes we are unable to fully grasp or understand what God is doing in our own life until we observe the dealing of God in the life of another brother or sister. And through our willingness to lay down our life for our friends, we learn a little more of Father's love and help to become administrators of His grace.

Through a Child's Eyes

"My daughter has a question to ask you." The daughter, a shy six year old, stood before the chair where I was sitting and stared at me with wide eyes as she grasped her mother's hand. This particular home meeting had been a bit unusual. After a time of song and praise, I had opened my mouth to begin teaching when I was pierced with the conviction that I had been selfish and discriminating in caring for others. As I began to confess these shortcomings to the 30 or so packed into the living room, I broke into sobs. Unable to continue speaking, I simply sat blubbering while the faces of the people became blurred through the tears. After what seemed to be about two weeks, I regained my composure and asked forgiveness of the people. The prayer and repentance that resulted was followed by expressions of joyful thankfulness. Now, as the mother and child stood before me, I wondered what such a young girl was so intent upon asking, but she continued to stare at me without saying a word. Finally her mother explained: "She wants to know what that light was surrounding your head."

I don't know what the little girl saw nor do I remember how I answered her, but I will never forget what was impressed upon my spirit. I believe that the Lord wanted me to know that true ministry can flow only from a place of brokenness and humility; that it is as we lay down our soul life for our friends that His glory is revealed and others are invited to eat of Jesus with us. I was not a pretty sight as I sat snotty-nosed with my insides hanging out before the people. It was about as comfortable as using the toilet before an audience of thousands. But that occasion and others like it taught me that looking good and preaching a dynamic sermon to huge crowds would accomplish little unless the life of Christ within me was being released through a broken vessel.

Leading Like Jesus

Jesus never managed anyone's life. Nor did He teach anything that was not illustrated by His own life. Rather, He invited those who would follow Him to "come and see." Those who took Him up on the offer saw where He stayed and how He lived. They saw Him communicate with His Father and eat with sinners. They watched Him respond to the harassment of the Pharisees and to the praise of some who heard Him teach. And as they walked with Him, He used simple illustrations to teach them how to stay connected with Father and to love one another in the face of these challenges. In short, Jesus led mainly by example. His life was open and vulnerable to all who were willing to "come and see."

Jesus never attempted to lead a large group of people. Though He sometimes taught and fed the crowds, there were only a few who actually walked closely with Him. And so it is today. Those who are on that journey sometimes need the touch of a more mature brother or sister to walk with them for a season as they grapple with the dynamics of life as a member of God's family. They need someone to love them through their times of failure and self-doubt; someone they can feel safe with. They long for someone who has become real and touchable to them because that person has invited them into their own life. They have at least heard about and most likely witnessed God's transforming power in the life of their friend. And as they have seen him or her follow after the heart of Father, they are encouraged to do the same. As they grow in Christ, they will find themselves leaning on the Great Shepherd in situations where formerly they would have sought out a human substitute. This way of leadership encourages a person to develop a trusting relationship with Father rather than to misplace one's dependence on another. Extending a leadership role beyond the temporary need retards growth and robs us of the joy of discovering Father's heart together simply as brothers and sisters.

A Strange Dream

Not long before I began writing this chapter, a woman called to tell me of a strange dream she had. The setting was a large room where people had presumably gathered for a church function. In the center of the room was a man who seemed to represent the pastor. He was completely unclothed, yet was evidently unashamed although everyone was staring at him. Most peculiar of all was that he had female parts where his male reproductive organs should have been. Finally he noticed the dreamer looking at him and he turned away embarrassed.

The dream might well symbolize the sad condition of many religious institutions of today.

Misplaced and thus impotent, they have little to give. Instead, they are continually seeking to draw resources to themselves while their adherents go hungry and the lost are left without the precious seed of the gospel. Though the Word is preached, the broken bread and poured out wine of the preacher's life is often missing.

Yet when a leader shares his moments of brokenness with those he walks with, it can be bread to those hungering for a satisfying relationship with Father. Jesus implored Peter to feed His sheep as an expression of Peter's love for Him. It would be safe to assume that he fed them with more than words before he made his final contribution as a martyr.

I must confess that I have suffered a great deal of mental anguish generated from my concern of what others thought of me. Often I would awake during the wee hours of a Monday morning regretting something I had said Sunday morning. Would the people still judge me to be just as capable a leader? Would the stupid remark detract from the high regard they had for me? I found myself searching for ways that I could be "transparent" without exposing the full extent of my selfishness. While hating the idea of being placed on a pedestal, I nevertheless clawed at the sides like a cat lest I should lose my perch!

The freedom and peace that comes from resting where I've fallen is a precious gift I will fight to keep. Inviting people to be a part of the good, bad and ugly of who I really am is helping to tear down the walls of separation that were built unintentionally by the religious class system I once served. How refreshing and nurturing it has become to "hang out" with brothers and sisters, equals, friends, to share our life in Christ together and to see Him more clearly because of it!

6

GATHERING AROUND
FATHER

"...When you come together, everyone has a hymn, or a word of instruction, a revelation, a tongue or an interpretation."

1 Corinthians 14:26

"We need a church in Sacramento like the one you were supposed to build. We now have a presence in New York and Honolulu, and we believe it's time for our type of church in Sacramento."

I hadn't heard the voice of my former network leader since I attended the wedding of a mutual friend several months prior to this surprising phone call. I left unsaid what I was thinking. *I thought God built His church His way. And why would anyone want their institutional presence when it's God's presence we're all celebrating? I wonder what "type" of church God builds?* He went on to say that he had heard our building was for sale (it wasn't) and wanted to know if his network could buy it. But as he talked on, I was finding myself mildly curious of what he would think if he knew how we were operating presently.

For the past year we had experimented with various ways of operating in a meeting environment that helped to redirect the focus from "up front" leadership to the reality of Jesus living and moving among us. We sought to encourage the free participation of all who gathered so that the teaching of the word, praise and worship, exhortation, etc., flowed from the body as a whole rather than from a select few. It followed naturally that the meetings moved from program to a more spontaneous nature, thus becoming less predictable. When I shared the word, I would generally take about five minutes to lay a foundation for the subject before inviting discussion.

It was often thrilling to see the word come to life through the unique contributions of the various ones who participated. At other times it was a bit frustrating when some tended to turn the focus on themselves or miss the point altogether. Yet overall, we were beginning to grasp the reality that whenever we gathered we were simply Father's kids taking another opportunity to love on Him and on one another. As such, we each had the opportunity to offer a valuable contribution towards the building up of the body. So what if someone spoke out of turn or prayed too long? These times together were not a production where a misstep could interrupt the carefully orchestrated flow of a flawless presentation. Rather, they were occasions to celebrate family around Father's table as we bragged on what Jesus had done all week long. In the process we were learning how to recognize and allow room for the work of the Holy Spirit as well as to receive one another with our various gifts and weaknesses.

Razing Routine

At times, prayer would be the main focus of a particular gathering, at others, body ministry. On some occasions, most of the time together was spent in praise and worship while the ministry of the Word was prevalent at others. Occasionally, worship, prayer, testimony and the ministry of the Word flowed together with such continuity that weeks of planning could not have produced the same result. On other occasions, I left the gathering feeling as though we had missed God altogether. Yet I knew that we could never go back to a structured "service" where a couple of us would decide what everyone else needs and thus serve it up to them in a neat package consisting of:

❖ Welcome (...*to the best church in town, where you will fit into our agenda for the morning. The Holy Spirit is welcome too, if we can figure out how to work Him into the program*)

❖ Opening Prayer (*what's being opened? If everybody's there, including the Holy Spirit, the gathering must already be happening*)

❖ Worship (*is this a warm-up or the main event?*)

❖ Announcements (*what you can't miss if you want to remain guilt-free*)

❖ Offering (*God loves a cheerful giver, but we'll take any kind.*)

❖ Sermon (*a lecture offering the opportunity to count how many pine knots there are per square yard on the ceiling directly over the cross multiplied by the estimated number of linear yards from front to back of sanctuary.*) followed by...

❖ Response Time (*Irma Jones, Thelda Drummonds and poor Teddy are at the altar for the 63rd Sunday in a row. Oh, well, looks good to the first time visitors*)

❖ Closing Prayer (*an advertisement for the next event that no one hears because they're thinking about lunch.*

Though I offer the above caricature with tongue in cheek, I suspect that many readers will readily identify with some of the comments.

Paul the apostle offers an instructive view of what should be expected when the church meets together. Yet one would be hard pressed to find even one of the elements he describes present in the Sunday morning meeting typical of most church gatherings of today. Even in the less structured meetings sometimes held during the week the congregants are rarely expected to come prepared to offer a song, a word of instruction, a revelation, etc., as described in 1Cor. 14:26–31. On the contrary, in most cases the leaders have carefully planned an event to move from one pre-determined segment to another while anticipating potential distractions with a planned response.

I wonder how often the Holy Spirit has engineered a distraction in an attempt to gain an audience for a least a moment or two!

Program Prison

We had sent a team to share the Good News in some remote villages in Mexico where the country folk were hungry for God. They would travel for miles on foot to pack out crude adobe buildings wherever the team was scheduled to minister.

One night Mark Newton was asked to be the first speaker of the evening, and, as it was his first time to accept such a responsibility, he was rather nervous. Just before the meeting was to begin he found himself in need of a restroom. Mark found a crude outhouse standing about 20 yards from the main building and went inside. His predicament became evident when he was ready to exit the tiny structure. He found no way to open the door from the inside! Push as he might, the little door held fast, and there was no opening through which he might reach the outside latch.

Mark could hear the shuffling feet and muted voices of stragglers passing the outhouse on their way to the meeting. Hoping to get help, he called out tentatively, using the only Spanish word he knew. "Holah!" ("Hello!") he said to the sound of approaching feet. No response. Becoming a bit frantic, Mark began calling out louder and less discriminately; "Holah, holah!" The locals, however, chose not to become involved with a foreigner yelling greetings from inside an outhouse!

Fortunately for Mark, someone finally became aware of his predicament and released him in time for his speaking debut. But I wonder how often Christ has been confined within our program far outside of the central place that should always be His and His alone. How often might He have attempted to interrupt our "form of godliness" to reveal His power? I shudder to realize that my own desire to keep the service "moving" was often the very thing that kept the Holy Spirit from doing so. For one thing, I failed to discern that Father could use others just as effectively as He could use me. I was certain I had the most to say and could say it better than anyone else!

I loved to preach and often thought that I could feel the anointing increasing along with the decibels. Nothing felt so good as being on a "roll", and at times the delivery of the word seemed so powerful to me that I could hardly believe the saints ability to remain so calm. Simply maddening was my observation that at the very peak of a powerful "preach" there were some whose drooping eyelids signaled a losing battle to stay awake! *My, I thought, how powerfully the devil fought to keep the word from getting through!*

Performing Pulpit

In the process of re-evaluation and research I learned that the Lord of the church never intended for preaching in a believers meeting to be a one-man affair. Most likely, preaching as is commonly practiced today did not even exist in the very early church. The Hebraic approach to life encouraged a practical application of biblical truth that rendered dialogue more effective than a lecture.

Even when Paul shared until midnight at Troas as recorded in Acts 20:7, the word dialogue (*dialegomai*) was used to indicate the participatory nature of the meeting. But the Greek's love of rhetoric, which placed the emphasis on the structure and style of what is taught, became the main teaching pattern of the church. As a result, preaching can become a performance to be enjoyed (or endured) for a moment and forgotten in the next.

On several occasions I have heard an admiring listener congratulate a speaker after a particularly rousing sermon by slapping him on the back while remarking, "You sure hit it out of the park today!" And most likely that is where it remained.

As long as we hold platform-based services "run" by professionals who are trained to perform, the focus of our meetings will be divided between God and those attempting to serve Him by managing His family gatherings.

7

SACRED SUNDAY SYNDROME

"Let us not give up meeting together as some are in the habit of doing, but let us encourage one another..."

(Hebrews 10:25 N.I.V.

"For where two or three come together in my name, there am I with them."

(Matthew 18:20)

The wide open spaces and jagged mountain ridges offered by the Arizona landscape seemed to clear the cobwebs from our minds as Rachel and I drove along a lonely highway toward our remote destination. We treasured vacation time. It was always an opportunity to leave behind the pressures and complexities of "ministry" to enjoy one another in a refreshing change of pace. Today, we planned to search out a historic ghost town that had fascinated me as a boy. Far off the beaten path, Sunnyside had been left unchanged since it was founded in 1902.

Finally, we turned off of the narrow highway and onto a dirt road. Eventually, the mesquite trees began to thicken and a few spruces could be seen as a hilly area came into view. Sensing that we were near our goal, I slowed the car and began to scrutinize the side of the road until a seldom used two wheel trail indicated the final leg of our journey. At last we pulled to a stop in front of an ancient barbed wire fence that seemed to have forgotten its purpose long ago. Not far beyond could be seen the tired wooden structures that once served as homes, a school house and a meeting facility for the community of Christians that had eked out a living from the harsh land a century earlier.

As Rachel and I began to explore among these rustic remains of the past, I noticed a white plume of smoke rising up from a wooded area about one hundred yards up the hill. Concentrating my gaze in that direction I could barely see the outline of a house through the trees. "Someone is living up there!" I exclaimed, surprised that anyone would have made their home so far from the comforts of civilization. The words had scarcely left my lips when two figures, seemingly transported from a bygone era, carefully picked their way down the hillside toward us, one leaning on the other for support. Clad in a wool suit coat and wrinkled slacks and sporting a long, white beard, a man in his eighties clasped the arm of his wife. She wore a 60's style smock-like apron over her blouse and trousers.

Another Blast From the Past

The old couple greeted us warmly and introduced themselves as John and Anna MacIntyre. We were fascinated to learn that they were original residents of Sunnyside. But the shock came when, after hearing my name, John knew who I was! He asked about my brother and sister by name and reminisced over incidents that took place in our childhood. Having been so young at the time of our acquaintance, I had long forgotten this dear couple.

Still, the surprises were not over. After learning that Rachel was born and raised in California, Anna shared about her relatives in the Visalia area of the same state. Incredibly, it turned out that my wife and this pioneer woman living in an Arizona ghost town were distantly related!

We hadn't chatted long before John and Anna invited us into their humble cottage for some more fellowship and a steaming slice of pumpkin pie that Anna had just extracted from her Franklin wood burning stove. We read an article from a 1900's edition of the New York Times that told the tale of the Christian community that had founded Sunnyside. We learned some interesting history about families I had known as a boy. But it wasn't long before the conversation turned towards John's favorite subject: his precious Lord and the passion of his heart to share Him with others.

I couldn't help but wonder why a couple with such a heart for the lost would live so far from another living soul. But then John's eyes shone even more brightly as he began to share of the wonderful opportunity that was his.

Apparently Sunnyside had become a favorite subject of historical research for certain colleges and universities. Left in its original condition and with undeveloped surroundings, such a relic offered a unique opportunity for students to observe and study a pristine example of a pioneer settlement. Once a week a different group of learners would visit the site at which John would be their guide. And week after week as he expounded on the rich history of the little town, he never failed to share the Secret of the community that was Sunnyside.

Where Two or Three...

As we shared the goodness of our Father together, Rachel longed to express her heart in music and asked if there was a piano in the house. Coaxing open a squeaky door to an unused room John indicated an ancient upright that had rested in silence for years. We gathered around the old forte while Rachel began to play an ageless hymn. As our voices blended in song, our hearts filled with wonder at God's unique blessings.

Only too soon, it was time for Rachel and me to leave. Gathering once more in the kitchen we joined hands and expressed our thanks to Father and asked His blessing to rest on one another. Finally, John's still strong baritone led us in singing "God Be With Us 'Til We Meet Again." The emotions we felt found their expression in tears that freely flowed from each of us .We knew how unlikely it was that the four of us would ever meet again on this earth, yet it was certain that the sweet fellowship we had shared would be a precious memory never to be forgotten.

* * *

In time, the free-style nature of the Sunday morning meetings in Sacramento became commonplace. Some older folks wanted the "anointed sermon" back, and the young people missed the guarantee of lively, instrument-led singing. Others cringed whenever certain individuals stood up to share and many were concerned that a small but significant number of the group remained spectators. Though everyone save for a handful had no desire to return to a "traditional" service, the earlier enthusiasm was all but gone.

Another concern was the lack of motivation among the group when it came to initiating fellowship during the week. On the other hand, they engaged one another so enthusiastically on Sunday mornings that one could scarcely gain their attention when attempting to move the meeting into another phase!

Finally, we took some time on a couple of Sunday mornings to dialogue as a church family regarding the situation. In the course of prayer and discussion we discovered that many were leaning on Sunday morning as their spiritual "fix." In fact, that once a week two-hour event had become the apex of their spiritual life! This in spite of the fact that the bulk of the teaching for the past several years was designed to achieve precisely the opposite goal! Moreover, even if several had shared a meaningful encounter with Father during the week, they felt that they hadn't "had church" unless they were present on Sunday morning where they may have spent the time distracted. So if a particular meeting failed to meet one's need, they felt cheated for the week!

"I'm in a tough work environment all week long," Roger explained, "so I come here to get my gas tank filled." Several others chorused their agreement with his sentiments.

It seems that Sunday morning had become a sacred cow. Rather than learning to *be* the church as we built up one another during the week we were still trying to "go to church". And Sunday morning in the "sanctuary" was the focal point of that illusion.

This is the Church, and This is the Steeple...

"Where do you *attend* church?"

"My church is *on the corner* of..."

"We have a super worship team *at* our church."

Familiar comments like these illustrate the fact that most people's notion of church is widely separated from what the New Testament leads us to understand church to be. Very few Christians would disagree with the assertion that the building they meet in on Sundays is not a church. Yet take away the building and many would conclude that "their church" had been "shut down".

Most would probably feel that the church was still operative if they met in homes on Sunday morning, and conducted services as usual as long as there was enough official leadership to preside over the meetings. However, they might feel that they had been reduced to a "home church." The very name implicates the place of meeting as essential to the nature of church. Yet a cursory examination of the early church as recorded in the book of Acts would seem to indicate that *where* and *when* believers met was of secondary importance at best. Whether gathering in a synagogue, in homes or in catacombs, their devotion to God, to one another, and to reaching the lost remained the essence of church life and expression.

They understood that God Himself was their sanctuary and that they both individually and corporately were His temple. The Chief Shepherd had promised them that whenever two or more of them met together He would be right there. So they went from house to house eating and worshipping together and releasing the overflowing, saving and miracle working power of God in the market place. It hardly seems likely that they spent much time or energy worrying about "church" buildings, attendance records or what would happen at the Sunday morning event!

Yet today, when Hebrews 10:25 is read: "Let us not give up meeting together, as some are in the habit of doing" the first thing that comes to most Christians' minds is Sunday morning.

The word used for "meeting" (*epi-sunagoge*) is simply the noun form of *sunago*, the verb Jesus used when assuring us that whenever two or three meet together He is in our midst. Still, most translations use the word "assembling." No doubt this choice of wording lends strength to the oft-held impression that a large gathering is indicated. Nowhere, however, does the scripture suggest that the number of people gathering, the place they meet or when they come together has any bearing on the significance or potential blessing of the occasion. Yet many conscientious believers feel guilty when they "play hooky" during the holy Sunday morning appointment with God.

Duty Bound

"Your landscaping is gorgeous!"

The unfamiliar female voice drew Ruth's attention from her garden tending to a friendly face beaming at her from the open window of a car that had come to a stop in front of her home on this bright Sunday morning.

"To tell the truth," Ruth answered, "I was feeling a bit guilty for skipping church this morning." *I don't want to be a bad witness to a neighbor who may not know Christ,* she thought. "Oh, I think this is probably where Jesus would be," came the cheerful response, and the lady smiled and waved as she drove away.

As Ruth thought about the stranger's words she became aware that her feeling of guilt was not the conviction of the Holy Spirit, but rather her inward response to what she felt was expected of a "good Christian." She was preparing the yard for her son's wedding reception and enjoying sweet communion with the Lord. At no time had she sensed that He was disappointed with her choice of venues. Yet the voice of religious obligation drawing strength from the traditional way of regarding "Sunday Church," intruded into an otherwise peaceful moment with Father.

So how did it come about, I wondered, *that after such a lengthy campaign to change our thinking regarding church, so many of us still seemed stuck in the Sacred Sunday syndrome? How had we become so entrenched in the traditions of men that the example of Scripture seemed to be of little effect?*

As we continued to search out the matter through prayer, study and dialogue, it became increasingly clear that the problem was rooted in an authority-generated church culture. This culture draws its breath from the disproportionate amount of energy, activity and focus directed toward Sunday morning in the "church" building. In so doing, it seeks to establish that event as the weekly spiritual climax for all who attend. This culture becomes so deeply ingrained in those who buy into the pastor's vision that even the scriptures are viewed through the cultural medium established.

Culture Shock

Perhaps a brief summary of the evolution of culture in this particular ministry would serve to illustrate the process that led us to the conclusion stated above.

When the leader of the network of which Rachel and I were formerly a part decided to start a church in Sacramento, the first priority was to find a suitable building in which to meet. When he found a great deal on a church facility that would accommodate approximately two hundred people, Rachel and I were asked if we would be interested in pioneering the work. We agreed, moved into the area and lived on a shoestring so that we could focus our time and energy toward helping to make the long-neglected facilities functional. Armed with the good fortune of a few handy and willing workers, we were soon able to set a date for the first gathering in the building.

On that first Sunday morning I shared "the vision" with the fifteen or sixteen people who were spread out on the first two rows. The vision was reinforced through preaching and printed material as the group expanded throughout the years.

After seven or eight years, we grew to two services on Sunday morning. One year later about a hundred people left. By the tenth anniversary of the church, Rachel and I were emotionally and physically drained. And while we had sought to encourage outreach and fellowship outside of the church facilities, most of our efforts had been poured into bringing the people into a building two or three times a week.

In James Thwaites' enlightening book, *Renegotiating The Church Contract,* the author offers a hypothetical example strikingly similar to our own story as recounted above. He uses it to point out what he sees as a problem with the way many churches are started and maintained. In the following quote, Tim is the pastor:

Ecclesiastic Domain

The key issue, to my mind, is that Tim has applied the name church solely to the activities he conducts within and from his building. In so doing, he has created a distinct ecclesiastic 'domain'. He has done this by drawing a social and psychological circle around a set of activities managed and overseen by himself and calling the things inside that circle 'church'. Tim has made a distinction between his 'domain' and the rest of what the saints are and do in life. He has assumed the right to name what he does 'church' and by implication has not permitted the saints to name what they do as 'church.' Hence the name, against which Jesus said the gates of hell would not prevail, has become contained in an organizational construct supervised by Pastor Tim.

Thwaite's comment brings to mind a remark made by Homer Simpson after helping some island natives build a chapel. Said he, "Well, I may not know much about God, but I have to say, we built a pretty nice cage for Him."

Being aware of the problem, however, accomplished little toward a solution. Though I continued to teach and encourage the people toward a different understanding, a large percentage of the group seemed unable to grasp the concept of church without Sunday morning in the building. As explained in Thwaite's example, I had spent the past ten years "making (my) church culture the dominant culture of the people who attend." Now I was discovering that my efforts coupled with the pre-existing traditional perception of "church" had become an almost insurmountable stronghold to overcome. Clearly, God would have to move in a way that would bring about the renewing of minds so that each individual would be able to receive the needed revelation for himself. I hardly expected him to move so suddenly.

8

OUT OF THE POND AND
INTO THE RIVER

Ruben ran here and there about the building taking photographs during one of our Sunday morning gatherings. This was his first visit to the states since we had begun working alongside several natives of Guadalajara, Mexico, where they reached out to abused women and children. Grinning from ear to ear he snapped another shot before joining me where I was standing near the back door. "This is a church without walls!" he exclaimed.

Certainly God had dealt with many of the fears and the religious "protocol" that had erected boundaries to the freedom that was rightfully ours. This new liberty was reflected in the joyful fellowship, passionate worship and readiness to express the gifts God had given us. Yet months later, the sense of discontent recorded earlier brought us to the realization that more change was needed.

During the week following our discovery of "sacred Sunday syndrome," many of us began to sense some definite leading of the Lord as we sought Him for further direction.

When we met again on a cool Sunday morning in early October everyone was quick to come to an agreement. We would not return to the building for a Sunday morning gathering for at least six weeks. After further discussion, we decided that we would come back together on the Sunday after Nancy, our missionary to Mexico, returned for a two month break. That would give us eight weeks to discover how life would play out without Sunday mornings in the building

Shedding the Old Wineskin

The sense of relief and freedom that washed over me as I drove out of the parking lot that morning was almost intoxicating. Although I had offered little direction to the meetings for many months, I was never able to shake the stifling sense of being responsible for whatever did or didn't happen.

I had learned by long experience that if I took control of the meeting, most everyone else would sit back for the ride. On the other hand, if I did nothing, too many people would follow my example. Though there were many times when the gatherings seemed powerfully led by the Spirit from "start to finish" I always felt frustrated and defeated when I judged them not to be. I hated showing up not knowing which it would be. Giving up control was no picnic. So that morning I felt as though I had just shed a heavy old coat that was two sizes too small. And I made a decision: I would not return to Sunday morning meetings on a regular basis again, regardless of what the group decided in eight weeks. I was done with *that* religious obligation for good!

As the days stretched into weeks, the people responded to the change in several different ways. A few began visiting other gatherings on Sunday mornings. Several others got together in a couple of different coffee shops, while some stayed home and watched football. Those that were worshipping and sharing the word at a care facility for Alzheimer patients every other Sunday morning continued to do so.

By the second week I lost track of what day it was until I retrieved the Sunday paper from its usual landing spot in the flower bed.

Most notable, however, was the effect that the missing two hours a week had on many people's relationship with the Lord. Some experienced an initial passivity toward pursuing the things of God. But many found that they were more motivated than ever to search the scriptures for themselves and to seek communion with Father. They reported a growing intimacy with Him on a daily basis and a greater ability to be spontaneous when sensing His leading on various occasions. Drawing moment by moment from the fountain of life that continually flows from a vital relationship with Christ was becoming a more evident necessity in the absence of the weekly trip to the watering hole.

Learning to Swim

It was almost as though we were learning to swim in the river rather than limiting ourselves to occasional visits at the pond! Of course, physical walls could never have the power to hinder the flow of the river of life in and through God's people. Yet the cultural boundaries that are often represented by "church" buildings can be strengthened in the environment where they are primarily introduced and maintained. And while Jesus at one point compared the Holy Spirit to a continuously flowing river, human nature will attempt to organize His functions and contain them within a structure. Sadly, too many rely on the "pond" for their water supply and tend to dry up during the week.

This is not meant to imply that the institutional structure is the only hindrance to a Spirit led life.

On the contrary, any aspect of our relationship with Father that we have confined to a certain time slot, place or set of circumstances is in danger of being reduced to a religious exercise. But the exaggerated importance placed upon the meeting in the building by most pastors serves to minimize the significance of the saint's daily life outside the walls.

I have often stepped out of my "prayer closet" after a glorious season in God's presence only to lose my peace when encountering the first distraction of the day! Incredibly, the transformation from spiritual giant to cowering dwarf was often completed in three seconds or less. My mistake was twofold.

First, I was under the illusion that rich, satisfying times with God served to change my heart and equip me for any eventuality. Feeling cleansed and full of faith and love, I would come away from my "quiet time" confident that I was ready to face the day. Unfortunately, I found myself surprised and disappointed by my fleshly response to various challenges. A familiar story from Peter's life may help to illustrate this dilemma.

A Pebble Confronts the Boulder

One warm afternoon Jesus and His disciples were resting near the foot of Mount Hermon on the outskirts of a paltry little town called Caesarea Philippi. Most of the group was sitting or reclining under the welcome shade of a willow tree, but Jesus stood with His back to them gazing toward the mountain's lofty summit. Still studying the mountain peak, He asked, "Who do people say the Son of Man is?"

"Some say John the Baptist," Nathaniel offered.

John adjusted the shoulder bag he was using for a headrest. "I've heard several speculate that you are Elijah; and still others, Jeremiah, or one of the prophets."

Suddenly Jesus turned to search the eyes of His followers. "Who do *you* say I am?" he asked.

The question seemed to ignite a flame of conviction in the depths of Peter's heart that overwhelmed every other thought in his mind. Rising to his feet he looked directly into his Master's eyes. "You are the Christ," he blurted, "The Son of the living God."

Jesus walked to where Peter stood and placed His hand on his shoulder. He spoke softly but with an intensity that commanded the undivided attention of every member of the group. "You are blessed, Simon, son of Jonah! This revelation didn't come from human wisdom or understanding, but directly from My Father in heaven."

Removing His hand from Peter's shoulder, Jesus stepped back and raised His voice.

"And I tell you that you are Peter, and on this rock I will build my church, and the gates of Hades will not overcome it. I will give you the keys of the kingdom of heaven, and whatever you bind on earth will be bound in heaven, and whatever you loose on earth will be loosed in heaven."

So overwhelmed was Peter by the Lord's declaration concerning him that he could hardly respond as Jesus warned the disciples not to tell anyone that He was the Christ. But when the Master went on to explain that He would soon suffer at the hands of the spiritual leaders in Jerusalem, where He would be killed and raised to life, Peter found his voice. Burning with righteous indignation and bolstered by a sense of new found authority he pulled the Christ, the Son of the living God, aside and began to rebuke Him!

"Never, Lord!" he said. "This shall never happen to You!"

Jesus turned and looked at Peter with an even greater intensity than before.

"Get behind Me, Satan! You are a stumbling block to Me; you do not have in mind the things of God, but the things of men."

Abiding Truth

From the "Rock of Revelation" with the keys of the kingdom to "Satan the "Stumbling Block" in one fell swoop! How could I so easily forget that meetings or even significant encounters with God, no matter how great the sense of His presence or how significant the revelation, do not, of themselves, change our basic nature nor equip us for our daily life? To be certain, they can and do serve as a catalyst for change if we allow the word received to take root in our lives.

Yet I have not been alone in the misconception that enough powerful meetings and revelations from God are the main fuel that propels the saint into the next "spiritual level." Many are the "Christian" commercials assuring us that a certain conference or meeting will "change our lives." And how many times has it been preached that God is going to "release the anointing that breaks the yoke"* in some "revival" meeting as if one blast from the revival gun is going to blow away the strongholds of the mind and disintegrate every hindrance to total victory?

Secondly, I thought that I would carry the presence of God from those special times throughout the day, drawing from them as

---

*This phrase is extracted from Isaiah 10:27 using the King James Version of the Bible. The NIV more accurately interprets the thought as put forth in the original language. Speaking of God's retribution against Assyria for their oppression of Israel, He promises them that "the yoke will be broken (from their neck) because you have grown so fat." The Hebrew words used here depicts the neck as a symbol of strength growing too large for the yoke to fit due to the strengthening gained from God's favor, lavished daily upon them.

though they were a spiritual bank account. This was a remarkable assumption considering that I had often studied, meditated and taught on the principle of abiding in Christ.

Our Daily Bread

A few days later when Peter, James and John experienced perhaps the most glorious engagement with God recorded in the New Testament, they were clueless as to the significance of what they had witnessed. They watched as Jesus changed into a Light Being before their eyes, while Elijah and Moses showed up to speak with Him.

But Peter's response completely missed the heart of God for this momentous occasion as well. He wanted to camp right there and build three private church buildings for Jesus, Moses and Elijah. This evoked an immediate response from Father God who nixed his suggestion by blinding them with a bright cloud. He reminded them that it was all about Jesus; He was the one they were to listen to!

Though any unique encounter with God or special time in His presence is certainly a privilege, it is our lack and His bounty that is most often revealed on such occasions. The moment we step out of the "pond" we find ourselves none the more "spiritual" for the experience. We are aware that every revelation must be lived out in our daily walk, yet we somehow imagine that the next "dip" will take care of our shortcomings. So many feel, like Peter, that if they could just stay in the "pond" they would become more like Jesus. So they increase their prayer time or run from meeting to meeting trying to keep "full of God". They end up leaning on meetings rather than on God Himself until they become exhausted and disillusioned.

It seems apparent that a significant need in Peter's life was for his mind to be renewed so that he could distinguish more clearly between his natural inclinations and the mind of the Spirit. But this comes only as we *respond* to the truth that He makes real to us by yielding our ambitions, desires and bodies to Father on a daily and hourly basis. Thus, the revelation of God and self that often occurs in any meeting with Father serves as a motivation and reminder to lean on Him more fully.

The sense of impotence that Peter and the other disciples must have felt on the mountain was doubtless repeated shortly after they entered the valley. Their inability to cure the epileptic boy further demonstrated their need to trust in Christ alone for the life and power that continually flowed from Him. Like the life-sustaining manna from heaven eaten in the desert by their ancestors, the life of the Bread from heaven could not be harvested in a glorious moment and stored for the following day.

The revelation on the mountain *did* lead to a conversation with Jesus on the way down to the valley where the disciples witnessed the Messiah's glory in action as the river of life continued to flow. But if the disciples counted on that singular meeting to carry them through the week, they must have been sadly disappointed by their impotence at the end of the day.

Learning Christ

It would be a serious mistake to minimize the significance of such encounters with God as those we have briefly alluded to in the previous paragraphs. Certainly these were spiritual landmarks in the lives of the disciples involved and include revelation upon which the Church of Christ is built and sustained.

Of most vital importance is that both of the encounters mentioned were orchestrated by God to reveal who Christ is. It is this revelation that is the very foundation of our faith, yet we can only see Jesus more fully as we yield to Him wholly in the common circumstances of every day. Still, I would be a poorer man if not for the special times I have been privileged to share with my Lord, both in meetings and alone with Him. And as I learn Christ on a daily basis, I will always welcome the next "mountain top" experience.

9

ENCOUNTERING THE COST

"For whoever wants to save his life will lose it..."

Mark 8:35

"Jesus...Who for the joy set before Him endured the cross, scorning it's shame..."

Hebrews 12:2

What Rachel and I encountered following the break from organized meetings played out to be the antithesis of a mountain top experience. I was not prepared for the season of intense emotional pain that was about to engulf our world. I had mistakenly assumed that the most challenging portion of the path we had chosen was behind us, but I was about to discover how wrong that notion was.

The course of events during this time seemed to parallel the portion of the trail still to be negotiated in the Hawaiian rain forest when we left the story earlier.

* * *

Navigating the comparatively easy portion of the trail allowed me to catch my breath before facing the steep precipice that had challenged me on the initial ascent. After arriving at the same 12 foot drop-off I had encountered earlier, I slithered down the thick rope thankful that on this part of the trail, at least, the same means used to climb up provided a way down as well.

Finally, I reached the embankment that I had been anticipating with so much foreboding. I stood on the edge of the precipice and studied the rocky surface of the steep embankment hoping to discover a promising route down to the dry wash below.

Spotting a section where exposed roots were within six feet of potential footholds as far down as I could see, I grabbed a vine and began a tentative descent, lowering myself from vine to root to mini-ledge. The almost tangible sense of relief that washed over me when at last my foot touched the canyon floor, was a tonic to my strained emotions and frayed nerves. I paused a moment just to relish the sense of restored peace and well-being and to thank God for His protection.

As I Anticipated rejoining the women shortly, I stepped onto the creek bed only to cry out in pain as sharp lava pierced my bare feet. I had forgotten that the one quarter mile back to the parking lot must be negotiated over a bed of jagged lava rocks! The vertical banks of the dry wash offered no alternative. Six inches of forward movement was accomplished with unbearable pain as the sharp edges of the lava rock threatened to slice my feet to shreds.

I gingerly lowered myself to a squatting position as I took a moment to muse over the irony of this latest predicament. Safe from the threat of falling to my death, I now had to choose between a crippling torture walk or wait for someone to come along and carry me out! My reflections were short lived, however, as the next attempt toward forward progress forced me to my knees offering two more victims to the lava spears. I thought of the flip flops that earlier had threatened my safety: now I was unable to go on without them.

For the third time since starting out on this "pleasure stroll," I prayed with a measure of desperation: "Father, I need your help again. Please make a way for me to get out of here before the women send out a search party."

I looked up to see a couple of well-muscled Samoan men making their way up the wash.

Balanced awkwardly on all fours and sporting scrapes and scratches from head to toe while a large camera equipment bag swung like a pendulum from my neck, I must have presented quite a spectacle for these tourist-weary locals. *Great,* I thought, *it must be my turn to provide these big boys with their visual dessert for the day.* They advanced toward me with measured steps while surveying my predicament with expressionless faces. *At least they're not laughing at me. Hopefully they don't have something more sinister in mind.*

Arriving at my side, one paused just long enough to slip off his flip flops and hold them out to me. "Take these," he said, "I don't need them." And the two stoic muscle men were gone before I finished saying "thank you."

I was never so grateful for such a simple gift and through a completely unexpected source, at that! One half inch of rubber separating my tender feet from the unforgiving lava bed transformed an impassable barrier into a roadway that would lead me safely to my goal.

* * *

The church Board was scheduled to meet several days before the end of the eight week hiatus from Sunday mornings in the building. At a meeting three months earlier, I had asked the Board to consider whether or not salaries should continue to be paid.

The church budget had been in deficit almost every month for some time, and that financial picture worsened as some folks moved on in search of a more predictable church environment. And though the present budget could still support one salary, there was a sense that God may have something else in mind.

Another item for consideration concerned the possibility that the church facilities no longer best served the needs of the body. The buildings were expensive to maintain, and we were using them less and less. Perhaps it was time to consider selling the property.

Not long after that meeting Amy, our bookkeeper, walked into my office with a big smile on her face. "I've decided to resign my salary," she said, "and continue my work on a volunteer basis." She went on to explain: "Somehow the minute I made that decision I felt so free I began to laugh. I don't know exactly why it is, but it seems as though an unhealthy connection to the organization was broken."

Since that day Amy, always a dedicated worker, has cheerfully labored well beyond the call of duty.

Deciding on Dollars

Several weeks before the Board was to meet again, I began to wrestle with the idea of laying down my salary as well, regardless of what the Board decided. Somehow, being a paid professional with wages set by the organization did not fit in with the way God was leading us. Other mature brothers and sisters in the group were as dedicated to the work of the ministry as Nancy and I, yet they were not being paid to be good Christians.

I realized that Paul, the apostle, supported the idea of providing for elders who did their work well, yet in the present context our salaried status seemed to set Nancy and me apart as having a more vital function than others in the body. This did not promote the understanding of brothers and sisters working side-by-side as equal members of a royal priesthood. Furthermore, I felt the need to be completely free of any obligation tied to receiving a salary.

Finally I realized that it was unfair to put the Board in the awkward place of having to make such a decision. This was neither their responsibility nor their burden to carry. This matter was between Father and me only.

About two weeks before the Board met, I made the decision to put aside my salary. The terms of severance would be left up to the Board to decide.

As we gathered for the meeting, a sense of solemn determination filtered through the usual light chatter that customarily preceded the coming to order. I wondered how my opening announcement would impact the five other members. Getting straight to the point, I informed them of my decision and waited for their response. Not one face registered signs of shock or even surprise. Nancy then proceeded to share her decision to lay aside her salary as well. Obviously, the Board members had each done their homework before the Lord and were prepared for what we had to say. Three of the members, having not discussed the matter among themselves, had already waited upon God for His will concerning a severance package. Each had come up with the same details regarding the terms.

Going, Going...Gone!

The second item on the agenda was the potential sale of the facilities. All six Board members were certain that we should sell. The final item we had put before the Lord concerned whether or not to resume Sunday morning meetings. Each member felt that the season for regularly scheduled corporate meetings was over.

What I had expected to be an intense, drawn out meeting had transpired quickly and smoothly. But still ahead was the reconvening of the whole church family on the coming Sunday. Although the entire group had been fully included in the decision-making process, it was hard to predict how such a radical proposal would be received.

Sunday, November 21st, 2004, marked a monumental day of decision for those who gathered at the Family Room for the first time in almost two months. They greeted one another with expectant hearts eager to discover what the immediate future might hold for this church family that had explored so much new territory together in the last few years.

As I began to share the conclusions reached by the Board, I searched the familiar faces of the faithful pioneers listening so intently. On each countenance was written the memories of the hard and joyous times we had shared along the way. I wondered how the decisions that would be finalized today would impact the lives of these dear people that I had grown to know and love.

I opened the meeting for discussion and was relieved to find that most of the people seemed to share the same conclusions as the Board. So in less than two hours a moratorium was set on the way we "had always done it." No longer would we gather Sunday after Sunday in this familiar setting where so many memories had been made, so many babies dedicated, weddings performed and sermons forgotten.

As Rachel and I left the building that day, I was thankful that this part of the transition was not nearly as difficult as I had anticipated. And although the future was uncertain, the freedom from the weight of what lay behind overrode any anxiety concerning what might lie ahead. Certainly this marked the beginning of a new era for Rachel and me and the brothers and sisters we walked with, and I was elated with anticipation of the adventure ahead.

But while I cheerfully abandoned the past and eagerly embraced the new, something altogether different was happening in Rachel's heart and mind.

Sharper than Lava

The changes over the last several months had affected a grave emotional toll on my precious wife. Although she embraced most of the things we were learning, she grieved over the loss of things she held dear.

As worship leader for many years, Rachel loved to express her heart in the music that flowed from her piano or keyboard along with the accompanying instruments. She thrived on the larger group atmosphere of celebration and weekly reunion.

During the week she worked part time in the office where she enjoyed creating the bulletin and planning various events. She was at the "nerve center" of all that went on and she poured her heart and soul into her work.

Now all this that had lent so much to Rachel's sense of purpose and identity was gone. Adding to the devastating feeling of loss was the shame she felt as the size of the group dwindled along with the finances. All we had tried to build was coming to nothing while our personal future was unknown. Rachel was sinking in a quagmire of despair.

One afternoon when trying to reason with her, I stuck my foot and most of my leg into my mouth. I foolishly questioned her willingness to respond to what God was saying rather than simply reaching out to her with compassion and understanding.

"You don't have a clue!" she cried. As all the pain and despair Rachel had been feeling for some time began to pour out of her, I realized that I was indeed clueless as to the depth of pain she battled. She continued: "I go to the piano and sing little songs like this:"

"I am worth nothing,
I am a zero.
I have no reason for living.
Please let me die, God, please let me die!"

I felt like someone had slammed my stomach with a sledge hammer. Heart-broken for my wife and constricted by fear for her well-being, I felt defeated and powerless to help her.

As I held Rachel in my arms, it seemed impossible to care about anything else. Had I failed to count the cost of following through with my convictions? I had just been praising God for taking us through the current phase of the journey with less difficulty than I had expected. Now, crushed by the grief and disillusionment my wife was suffering as a result of my decisions, it seemed too painful to attempt another step on the hazardous path we had taken.

In the Arms of the Good Shepherd

Later that day I cried out to Father in anguish. "What have I done? Please touch my wife and restore her! There is no joy in going on when the one I love so dearly is suffering so severely. I will obey you, Lord, but I really don't want to."

In the midst of my pain and confusion I seemed to hear a still, small voice reminding me of the many times I had begged the Lord to have His way with us no matter what the cost. I had just finished teaching a fifteen hour *Crossroads* class at Youth With A Mission on the cost of discipleship. Some of us had wept as we considered the cherished privilege of sharing in the fellowship of our Lord's suffering. In such a moment, the loss of position, prestige, reputation and financial security seemed but a trivial price to pay in contrast to the unfathomable sacrifice of the Son of God. Yet, "He endured the cross and scorned its shame" for the joy that would come as a result of His obedience. In the light of such incredible love, mentioning "cost" seemed almost impertinent.

Now in my grief over Rachel's agonizing despair, I came to realize that even this was but a fleeting sting not worthy to be mentioned in light of the wonders of Father's love yet to be revealed. The harsh reality of Rachel's pain did not go away. Still, the love of Father demonstrated through the comfort of His Spirit was like a buffer between my tender feet and the treacherous path that would lead us both closer to Him. It was just like Jesus to meet us on the way and offer me His shoes while He promised to carry Rachel in His arms.

10

DIRT, DREAMS AND DOLLARS

"So do not worry, saying, 'What shall we eat?' or 'What shall we drink?' or 'What shall we wear?' For the pagans run after all these things, and your heavenly Father knows that you need them. But seek first His kingdom and His righteousness, and all these things will be given to you as well."

Matthew 6:31–33

"We've got a flood out here!"

The urgent cry instantly broke through my subconscious state, and sent Rachel and me scrambling down the stairs to join my 80-year-old mother, where she stood staring at the disaster in our front yard. In the early morning dusk we could see that water was gushing from an irrigation main, and had covered the patio and entryway several inches deep. We soon learned that the overflow had seeped under Mom's front door into her apartment, where it was soaking the newly laid carpet.

The women ran to grab buckets and brooms, as I shut off the main water valve that supplied the new sprinkler system. I groaned at the prospect of re-doing even a small part of a project that had consumed most of my time and energy over the last two months.

Before we sold the church facilities, I had met up with a former acquaintance who agreed to hire me as a salesman for a sun shade company of which he was part owner. I was not scheduled to begin working for a couple of months, however, so I began re-landscaping the front yard of our house. This project involved rockscaping, ripping out old lawn, replacing a concrete driveway with sod, removing six trees, constructing a path with pavers to descend 3 feet from the street, and installing an irrigation system. Finally, I would level a 10 by 12 foot area, and lay a patio using artificial stone pavers to match the meandering path. The final touches would involve the replacement of varied greenery before spreading a couple tons of gravel.

The job turned out to be even more challenging than I had anticipated. Day after day for over 9 weeks I tumbled out of bed, reached for a mud stained outfit, and attacked root-bound clay with my trusty shovel. Eventually I developed tendonitis in both wrists, and began to lose sleep. But the most challenging moments for me occurred when I had to re-do a difficult task for which I lacked sufficient knowledge. I began to develop an attitude whenever encountering a setback to progress.

Another Session with the Violin

Bottom line, I was beginning to feel sorry for myself. After all, I had given up a comfortable salary and a white collar position, where everyone admired me and wanted to serve me. Now it seemed that I spent most of the time with my head in the dirt and my rear end in the air like a stink bug.

Moreover, my shoes had the uncanny ability to attract dog deposits like a magnet. Incredibly, I seemed incapable of spotting the offending morsels when picking my way across the lawn. If I ventured into the back yard to enter the tool shed, I invariably left with the treads of my shoes filled with a fresh sample.

The redundancy of my predicament was infuriating to me, while providing rich dessert for my daughter, who was often visiting her mom as I was playing in the soil. Mumbling to myself while dragging a tiny stick through each tread line, I could see Lauryn thrashing around on the living room floor overcome with paroxysms of laughter.

One day after a similar incident, I lifted my dirt-encrusted hands to God, and cried out in frustration: "Is this what my life has come to... dirt, poop and frustration? What are you wanting to teach me through all of this?"

The answer would come slowly over the next couple of weeks. Since beginning the landscaping project, I had scant opportunity to touch the lives of those with whom my own life had for so long been involved. And although several of the men who I have walked with were quick to help me on weekends, I had spent more time alone since starting the job, than ever before. Ministering to the body of Christ around the world seemed to be a thing of the past. It became clear that I was being stripped of much that contributed to my sense of self-worth. Yet another challenge was still to come.

The completion of the landscaping coincided nicely with the projected start time for the sales position I had been offered with the sunshade company. I saw this opportunity as a gift from God, because it offered the potential to establish a comfortable income, while allowing the flexibility to pursue His leading in other areas. But when I called my future boss, he informed me that they could no longer use me, as the company was undergoing an unusual slump in business.

I had no idea of what I could do to support my family. Having researched the possibilities earlier, I found little available for a man of my age, who had no job experience other than that of "pastoring" for the previous 30 years.

Now, as I swept water toward a corner drain, the moment served to illustrate what was happening to my sense of personal value. The path I chose had already cost my wife dearly. The prospect of no apparent job opportunities waiting in the wings could hardly add to her sense of security and well being.

I already felt as though I had little to offer the family of God. Now it seemed as though my ability to contribute to my natural family was going down the drain as well. Although encounters with dog deposits, job set-backs and strained tendons were superficial annoyances, each incident seemed to be mocking my trust in Father to work out the deeper issues for good.

Reduced to Love

It was during this season that Father began to reveal an aspect of His nature through my wife. Rachel was delighted with the new front yard, and often led me out onto the patio where we would sit together for a half hour or so in the morning. She seemed to treasure our moments together more than ever, and would express her love and appreciation for me in tender ways. It was obvious that her regard for me was not based on my ability to provide her with an easy life or a comfortable income. She loved me for me, and she responded to my love for her.

There was simplicity in her outlook that appeared to have emerged out of the shattering of her original hopes and dreams. She was no longer trying to live up to a standard, or to measure her approval rating by her performance. She was confident only that God is good, and that He loves. She decided to leave the rest up to Him.

Rachel's child-like attitude helped me to see that Father was simply working to "reduce" me to love. I thought I had already learned that His love for me was not based on my performance, but my emotions revealed that I had separated my sense of value from His love. One truth began to strike home. I was valuable because He loved me. I was called *to* Him, not to perform *for* Him. This was another simple truth that I had often taught, but never realized fully on an experiential basis. And it was an understanding that enabled me to hear something from Father's heart that I would not have been able to receive previously.

The Money Question

One morning I was sharing my concerns regarding employment with Him, and asking for direction for the days ahead. The answer impressed on my spirit could hardly have been more clearly indicated if He had spoken in an audible voice. *Pursue your dreams. Don't obligate yourself to a job with set hours and schedule. I have not released you from the work I have called you to do. Do what I tell you to do, and I will provide.* This affirming direction revived my spirit, and filled me with joyful anticipation. However, the immediate sense of peace was soon challenged by the fear that I could be stepping out on presumption rather than on faith.

Two weeks later I was beginning to question the validity of the direction I had sensed so keenly was from Father. I recalled the sad state of some I had known who said that God had called them to live "by faith." Their interpretation of that directive had resulted in the financial ruin of their family. I have always had a strong work ethic, and despised the philosophy and lifestyle of some who used "ministry" as an excuse to default in their responsibility to provide for their families. Having begun my first full-time job digging ditches under the Arizona sun, I have always believed that one must do whatever it takes to provide. Although I have witnessed miracles of God's provision for my family when we lived on a nearly impossible budget for a season with Mobile Ministries, the memories of "scraping by" are not fond ones for my wife.

It was during this wool gathering session that I received a phone call from a good friend and co-worker in Flagstaff, Arizona. "I intended to call you a couple of weeks ago," Mel began, "but I was hesitant to share, because it is about a dream I had. After all, it could just be a result of too much pizza the night before. Anyway, in the dream Jesus was talking to me about you. He said that you should not get tied down to a regular job, and to remain mobile, available to respond to however He might lead you. He promised to provide your needs."

At this point I told Mel what I had sensed that Father had been saying to me during the time he had the dream. When I mentioned the part about pursuing my dreams, he broke in excitedly: "That's it!" he exclaimed, "That's exactly what he said to me in the dream as well!"

I must admit that it took several other confirmations before I came to terms with the idea that I might never be sure of how the next means of provision would come. But it wasn't long before God began to demonstrate His faithfulness to His word.

Creative Financing?

It had never occurred to me to consider counseling professionally until some dear friends had stopped by one day. Darrell and Ann Barrett had been trained in biblical counseling through a program we had offered at the church facilities several years previous. Now they were counseling out of their home, and enjoying the opportunity to touch people's lives in a meaningful way while supplementing their income as well. Darrell asked me if I had ever considered doing the same.

The idea seemed to make sense. It would offer a way to present the love and truth of God to those who had never come into a relationship with Him, as well as an expanded opportunity to touch the lives of His children. At the same time, even if I offered fees below the usual rate per session, I would be averaging four times the hourly income offered by other jobs I could qualify for. This would make it possible to remain flexible with my time, and thus available for whatever else God had included in His plans for me.

After sensing a go-ahead in my spirit from Father, I soon had liability insurance coverage and a certificate on the office wall. But the new telephone books would not be published and distributed for several months. In further conversations with Darrell and Ann, I learned that the Yellow Pages advertising would most likely attract a minimal number of clients. It was clear that this new venture would only account for a small portion of the income that I needed to survive financially, until a clientele base could slowly expand over a period of time.

One morning I was strolling through a high school football field in our neighborhood after various forms of advertising I had tried all failed to produce a single client. I was struggling with the decision of whether to spend more of our dwindling supply of finances on more high powered advertising. Finally, I decided to ask, what for me, was an unusual request of the Lord. "Father," I said, "I don't want to spend time, energy and money on something that you have not chosen to be the principal way of provision for our family. Would you please show me *today* how you intend to provide for us?"

That afternoon I opened the mail to find a check for six hundred dollars from a young couple who were unaware of our need. A day or so later, I called the bookkeeper so that she could record their gift. She mentioned that some other checks had come in for us over a period of time that she had forgotten to give to us. When I opened the consolidated check her husband handed me, I was stunned to read a figure of several thousand dollars!

The Carefree Life

Over the next several months, money came in from unexpected sources, including people who have never before given to us or the organization we had represented. Rachel's part-time bank teller's job has provided supplemental income, and the few clients that have come for counseling since the

Yellow Pages were published have been a blessing as well. But it is clear that Father's plan for us is to depend on Him alone for our source of provision.

We still have no way of knowing how He will provide in the future, but we are confident that He will.

Do what I tell you to do, and I will provide. These are the words that remain at the forefront of my mind as each new day unfolds. Sometimes most of the hours will be spent writing. On other days various chores, errands or counseling sessions will fill most of the daylight hours. But whether driving my mother to the doctor's office or taking an afternoon just to hang out with my wife, I'm learning that it is all strategic toward receiving of Father's super-abundant supply. My primary focus of responsibility has shifted from "what I must do to make sure that I am providing for my family," to learning how to respond to Father with the confidence that He will provide as I trust Him on a day to day basis.

Recently I met a younger man who had begun a very similar journey to ours just several months before this writing. As we chatted in a crowded coffee house, Jason (not his real name) began to share the struggle he was having with the direction he felt he was to pursue after resigning his position as senior pastor. Motivated to seek a good paying job to provide for his wife and children, he felt that God had challenged his initial intentions. Now he felt impressed to further his education.

As I began to share with him the way Father was working in my life, Jason made an insightful comment. "It sounds like you're saying that God is bringing us into the understanding of how to enter the care-free life."

I agree whole-heartedly with Jason's summary of the way Jesus said we are all called to live. To never worry about what we will eat, drink or wear, or about what tomorrow might bring, is certainly a carefree way to live. Yet that is the attitude He said we should have if we are making kingdom things our priority.

I still have moments when a slight pang of anxiety will disturb my peace after an unexpected expense arises. And there are times when I allow financial considerations to override the still, small voice of the Spirit when making a decision. But to the degree that I approach each day with a child-like trust that Father will provide, I am finding life to be less stressful and much more enjoyable. And it's certainly a much greater adventure!

I am not suggesting, of course, that the more usual means of employment should be abandoned for a lifestyle in which the source of the next day's provision is every evening's mystery. To do so without clear direction from God would be folly. Furthermore, as we will see in an upcoming chapter, the workplace is most often the venue where Father seeks to establish the kingdom through His children.

What Father is helping me to learn, is that provision for my family is His responsibility when I am employed according to His direction. And, in fact, everything I might worry about is taken care of as I cast my cares on Him and respond to His leading.

11

ROCKING BACK

"My soul finds rest in God alone; my salvation comes from Him. He alone is my rock and my salvation; He is my fortress, I will never be shaken."

(Psalm 62:1–2)

"Because your love is better than life, my lips will glorify you. Because you are my help, I sing in the shadow of your wings. My soul clings to you; your right hand upholds me."

(Psalm 63:3,7,8)

It was a seasonably warm night in Failsibad, Pakistan where a small missions team from the U.S. had been invited to minister to several church gatherings. On this particular evening I was scheduled to address a group of about four hundred believers who assembled at the dead end of a street in a typically crowded suburb. Scattered among them would be Islamic spies who would take note of any who might openly confess Christ or otherwise break one of their religious laws. The believers knew that without the protection of a building, the risk of attack by hostile Muslims was even greater, but their hunger was greater still.

Guarded by two tough-looking ex-Taliban believers armed with an Uzi and a sawed off shotgun, I stood to address the crowd whose faces registered a mixture of caution and intense expectancy. I had been warned not to mention Israel, Jerusalem, India or the United States. Most importantly, any unfavorable comments regarding Islam would undoubtedly result in serious consequences.

Feeling bold and passionate, I took my message to the limits, stressing salvation through Christ alone and proclaiming every religion false that taught otherwise. Lifting my Bible high while declaring it to be the only book with divine authority, I made a clear target with a white sheet used as a backdrop directly behind me. Meanwhile, the other team members were slouching as low as possible in their chairs as angry Muslims began creating a stir. The threat was quickly resolved by our armed companions, and the rest of the meeting resumed without incident.

I must admit I was feeling pretty good about my fearless presentation of the gospel until the next afternoon when we met Salima. As our host shared her story, my ego was deflated while my heart filled with wonder at the sustaining grace of Father God.

Salima's Secret

At sixteen years of age Salima could not keep her newfound relationship with her loving Father to herself. She gave a Bible to a friend who found the key to life in the pages of the forbidden book. Unable to convince his daughter to denounce Christ, her father took Salima's friend to a remote area and shot her to death.

The terrible disgrace was now removed from his family, but the death of his daughter had to be avenged. Having given her friend the Bible, Salima was held responsible for the murder. She was taken to prison where the guards tortured her for two years while demanding that she denounce Christ and re-convert to Islam. They pushed chili peppers into the corners of her eyes and forced them up into her vaginal tract. One day, they brought Salima's pastor into her cell. The guards stripped them both naked and tried to force them into sexual compromise. When they refused, the guards hung the pastor by his feet and beat him until his collar bone and ribs were broken. Kissing the cross that she wore around her neck Salima declared, "I will never deny my Jesus!"

Our host happened to be ministering in the United States when he heard what was happening with Salima. He shared the story on two of the most widely viewed Christian television shows in the nation to solicit the prayers of thousands of Christians. When he returned to Pakistan, the Lord intervened with an unprecedented series of events that led to Salima's release shortly before we arrived.

When our host concluded the story, we sat in somber silence for a moment humbled by the dedication and courageous spirit of the petite, eighteen year old girl who stood serenely before us. Finally, one of us asked a question that most certainly weighed on each of our minds.

"Salima, how were you able to withstand such merciless torture for these past two years?"

Salima gazed steadily back at us with a look of understanding that seemed to open a window into the soul of one who had discovered priceless treasures in a mysterious and forbidden place that we had never visited.

"The Holy Spirit gave me love songs to Jesus," was her simple answer.

We asked Salima if she would sing one for us. She smiled her assent and began to sing in a hauntingly beautiful voice as her face became radiant with love for her Lord. Although we were unable to understand the words, the sense of Father's love was so strong that tears coursed down our faces as we were humbled in His presence.

"All I want is to serve my Jesus and reach my people."

We asked Salima what we could do for her. She replied that she did not want to seek safety in the United States nor did she need lots of money; she just wanted to dedicate her life to reaching her people.

When I had preached on the street with such bravado the night before, I had been surrounded by my companions, protected by armed body guards and would soon be headed back to my family and friends in a free country. My confidence in God's protection was supplemented by a human support system.

But Salima had found that God *alone* was her strength, her hope and her salvation. He *alone* could meet her need in the most dire of circumstances and even be her joy in the darkest hour. While living under the shadow of death, she could sing in the shadow of His wings, for she clung to Him who alone was her help. To her, His love was better than life. Salima was satisfied with Jesus

* * *

When we discontinued the regular gatherings, some of the people found it difficult to stay in touch with those they used to see as often as two or three times a week. They became even more aware of their dependency on meetings to fill their spiritual gas tank rather than to drink deeply of Christ on a daily basis.

But they also began to discover that they had been leaning on brothers and sisters to satisfy emotional needs that Father Himself was longing to fulfill.

"It's all Jesus!" I had to hold the cell phone away from my ear as Lynn practically screamed in her enthusiasm. "It's not about needing people or going to meetings, it's all Him; He's all I need!"

Vivacious, outgoing and loving to serve, Lynn found herself making the 30 mile trip from her house to the Family Room more often then some who lived just a few blocks away. Lynn had been abused as a child and grew up feeling inferior to and rejected by other members of her family. Although her husband, Jerry, was affirming and supportive, her need for acceptance and affirmation was a crucial issue in her life.

As might be expected, her "spiritual family" became an important ingredient toward fulfilling that hunger. During times when Lynn was feeling insecure, her connection with those she felt close to was like a lifeline to her.

Now, in the absence of the regularly scheduled meetings Lynn began to feel a vacancy in her life. Although she communicated with her friends by phone and took advantage of opportunities to get together, the limitations caused by distance took a toll on the frequency of the fellowship she thrived on.

But soon Lynn began to notice something else stirring within her. "I sensed that God was jealous for my undivided attention," she told me. "I began to realize that as precious as the fellowship with my brothers and sisters is, it could never fulfill the deep heart need that was always with me. As I pressed into God more and more, I began to experience love and acceptance such as I had never imagined. I had always been insecure even in my closest relationships, but when I began to realize that God's love for me was undaunted by my weakness and failure, I became less concerned by what others might think of me."

Lynn came up for air before she continued, "I understand now that God had to separate me from people to a certain extent so that He could teach me that He alone is my strength, security and fulfillment. Before coming to know Him in that dimension, my relationship with people was unbalanced and forever disappointing my expectations."

Satisfied with Jesus

Lynn was learning a truth that I had found hard to accept when I first heard it verbalized by my friend, Wayne Jacobsen. "We don't need fellowship," he said, "We only need Father, but we get to have fellowship!"

Obviously, fellowship with other believers is vital to the building up of the body of Christ and, as such, constitutes a need so far as the Church is concerned (see 1Corinthians 12:21). Yet every believer has the privilege of finding God alone to be more than enough, whether banished from society or surrounded by faithful friends. And so we can say of the All Sufficient One, "He alone is my rock and my salvation, my hope and expectation. He is my shield and exceeding great reward, my glory and the lifter of my head. He is a friend that sticks closer than a brother, my counselor and guide. He's bread from heaven, water from the rock and comfort in the storm. He's my apostle, prophet, evangelist, pastor, teacher, helper and healer... He's all I need."

And if He is all this to me, I can receive the gifts He's given to the church and give myself as well. For the revelation of who He is constitutes the only foundation for true relationship in His body. If He is all sufficient for each of us, how freely we can serve one another! How free we can be from the fears and false expectations that would taint the purity of the gift that Father has given to us in one another! I am so thankful for my brothers and sisters in Christ. But I am satisfied with Jesus!

12

THE FAMILY FACTOR

"For this reason I kneel before the Father from whom His whole family in heaven and earth derives its name. I pray that out of His glorious riches He may strengthen you with power through His Spirit in your inner being, so that Christ may dwell in your hearts through faith. And I pray that you, being rooted and established in love, may have power, together with all the saints, to grasp how wide and long and high and deep is the love of Christ, and to know this love that surpasses knowledge that you may be filled to the measure of all the fullness of God."

(Ephesians 3:14–19)

"...so in Christ we who are many form one body, and each member belongs to all the others."

(Romans 12:5)

When Rachel and I were newlyweds, I was such a private and selfish individual that I begrudged sharing an evening at home with friends. I seriously considered forgoing a telephone service so that my mother-in-law would be unable to vocally intrude at will! I was uncomfortable if I thought someone was watching me eat and strictly refrained from expressing any emotion in the presence of anyone but immediate family. In short, I was as generous as Scrooge and as vulnerable as a lead box.

Before meeting Rachel, I had secured immigrant status and passage to Australia where I knew I would find more wilderness than people. This plan was no small concession to my original intention which had been to homestead deep in the Canadian wilderness where I would live off the land. The drought of members of the opposite sex eager to share the experience, however, soured that little dream.

And now that Rachel and I were married, my hopes for a sequestered life were shattered when I learned that the Australian government would not permit Rachel to accompany me "down under" unless she became an immigrant as well. As our ship was to sail well before her immigration papers could be processed, I was struck with the brilliant revelation that just maybe God was tracking somewhere else with this whole idea. We moved to San Jose, California, and set up housekeeping.

A Baptism of Love

Four years later I became deeply dissatisfied in my relationship with God and hungered for the joy I saw in some of my Christian friends. One night a familiar verse of scripture seemed addressed to me personally: "Seek first the kingdom of God and His righteousness, and all these things will be added unto you." "Lord," I prayed, "maybe I will never know the joy and life that some of my buddies seem to have, but because You are worthy, I will serve You with all my heart from this day forth."

A couple of days later I was driving home from my job as a landscape estimator when I felt driven by an intense urge to pray. When I arrived home, I bolted for the bedroom, shut the door and fell to my knees by the bed. I became keenly aware that the Holy Spirit was moving within me to expose the attitudes and disposition that kept me from receiving all that He longed to give. For the next 30 minutes or so he made it very easy for me to yield right-of-way to Him as He loved me while I sobbed like a baby. Just when I thought He was through I was filled with joy and laughter such as I had never before experienced. The tears continued to flow even as the laughter bubbled up like a fountain.

For the next few days, Father's love seemed almost tangible to me. I would no sooner sit down on the couch when it seemed as though Father sat down beside me to put His arm around me. Silently, tears of joy would start to flow again. Rachel, busy preparing dinner in the kitchen, would suddenly drop what she was doing, walk into the living room, plop down beside me and throw her arms around me.

I was soon to find that it is to the degree that we learn to daily walk with Jesus in the joyful freedom that Father made possible through His abundant forgiveness, unfailing love and full redemption, that we are able to cultivate healthy relationships in His family. The way we receive from Him is the manner in which we will give. And as we give of ourselves to others, it is given to us "pressed down, shaken together and flowing over" so that we are able to grow in the scope and depth of the relationships that Father blesses us with.

It was not long before the Lord provided an outlet for the love He was pouring into me. That was when Rachel and I became involved with Mobile Ministries, the group described in the last few pages of Chapter 2. Suddenly, Mr. Isolationist found himself living in the fastest growing city in the world and surrounded by people of every age, shape, size and background! Soon we lived in one of five homes where people came and went at all hours of the day and night while the phones rang incessantly and privacy was measured by the length of time in the bathroom determined by the business at hand.

Stretching Exercise

It was not difficult to see how God was using this challenging environment as a tool to confront my narrow boundaries and to stretch my capacity to love and accept others. He was about to use community as a potter's house where a shaping process would commence toward creating some of the characteristics of leadership introduced in Chapter 5.

Although Rachel seemed to roll with the punches, I fought for small areas of "turf" that I could call my own. This was no small task as we never knew what homeless person or family might be living with us during any given week or month or what dynamics they might introduce to the household.

One of our guests had escaped from a psychiatric hospital where she was usually kept in a padded cell because of her violent nature. Another was a mentally ill man tortured by guilt who would sometimes awake us in the middle of the night with his terrifying scream: "I'm going to heeeellllll!" One mentally handicapped woman practiced no personal hygiene and would soil her hands after using the toilet. Of course she loved "my" particular brand of crackers and would freely thrust her unwashed hands into the box as I cringed in horror.

Frank (not his real name) was an ex-convict just released from prison. He was pleasant enough and thankful for a place to stay, but was plagued with the thought that his fiancé would soon be released as well, and he had no way to provide for the two of them. He seemed to think that I held the key to a solution and followed me around like a lost puppy.

It was my habit to eat breakfast early when I could enjoy the meal in peaceful solitude. With Frank's arrival, however, this little reprieve was quickly censured. I would not make it to the cupboard where the cold cereal was kept before hearing a chair being drawn up to the table where Frank would be waiting for me with his cup of coffee. As I would sit down and begin to eat, his mournful eyes studiously searched my face, as if he expected me to spot his fortune in the cornflakes at any moment.

Determined to regain my morning oasis, I began to vary my breakfast time. Tiptoeing down the stairs at an early hour and creeping into the kitchen I would carefully open the cupboard and withdraw the cereal box with noiseless precision. But either Frank had the ears of a fox or he never slept. Starting from his bed on the couch as though responding to a gun shot, he would sprint into the kitchen and resume his stake-out at the opposite end of the table before my cereal was poured!

Choosing to Love

I finally realized that I had a choice to make: I could continue to fight a losing battle for the preservation of my personal comfort zone or allow God to teach me how to love the people He was putting in front of me with even a fraction of the love He so freely poured on me. I had to face the fact that, although I loved to spend time alone with God, I resented His habit of inviting His friends to invade my life. Yet I read in 1John 4:20 that "anyone who does not love his brother, whom he has seen, cannot love God whom he has not seen." I cringed to think that the intimacy I enjoyed with God was based in sentiment or, at best, a shallow understanding of what love really is. Giving wise counsel was always fulfilling and rewarding, but working it out in my own life was painful and costly.

Driving across town at 2 a.m. to force warm salt water into an overdose victim to induce vomiting is no picnic; sharing personal time and opening up my own life to those not of my choosing proved to be an even greater challenge. Whether it was a needy, new convert or a "seasoned" brother or sister with a difficult personality that seemed to want a piece of me, I drew the line between "ministry" and friendship.

I found it much easier to belong to an institution than to another in God's family. It took less commitment to be planted in a place than to be rooted and grounded in love. And if feeling challenged to give more of myself, I would remind myself that the apostles separated themselves to the ministry of the word and prayer. Besides, some wanted to be close to "leadership" just to feel important. Certainly it was not God's will for one to encourage relationships based on such spurious motives! How convenient it can become to spare oneself an undesired relationship by stamping God's endorsement on our decision!

When my daughter, Lauryn, was about four years old she loved to play "horsy" with her grandfather. One Sunday afternoon "Papa" scurried around the family room on all fours doing his best to simulate a bucking bronco while Lauryn tried to stay on his back. As she giggled and screeched with glee, it was hard to tell who was having the most fun! But when the "horsy" inadvertently passed gas with a powerful punch, Lauryn slowly climbed down and took several steps backward. "Papa" excused himself to the restroom but returned in a minute and again dropped enthusiastically to all fours eager to re-engage his granddaughter in their favorite game. But Lauryn had decided the stakes were too high. Remaining at a safe distance, her little face was solemn as she said: "Papa", I don't think God wants us to play "horsy" anymore."

Priority Connection

Like father, like daughter! But now in the communal environment to which I had committed myself and family, it became obvious that God was choosing my friends for me. And as I began to relax the boundaries I had erected to keep some from getting too close, a wonderful thing started to happen. I actually began to *enjoy* the company of some who I had once considered an annoyance.

But still more significant was the discovery that connecting in heart with one of Father's kids seemed to open my own heart to receive from Him more fully! On several occasions when I had set aside time to be alone with Him, I felt a lack in the sense of communion we normally shared. Feeling prompted to touch bases with a certain brother or sister, I would do so to find that when I resumed the "alone" time with Father, the sense of His love and presence was especially sweet.

This has been my experience from time to time ever since. And though He often reveals precious secrets in those "alone" times, a more complete wisdom seems to be revealed when sharing life in Christ with others to whom our hearts are joined. It's as if He would remind me that though He alone is my rock, he is also "our" Father.

We must be primarily and intimately connected to Him in order to be rightfully connected to one another, yet both connections must be maintained if we are to enjoy the fullness of His goodness and wisdom (Colossians 2:2,3). Obviously, the additional wisdom, gifting and peculiarly individual relationship with God that each has to offer when we come together helps to make this true. Yet beyond that, the organic nature of our union with Christ and one another seems to open a flow of His grace that waters our soul as we prefer one another in love.

Loving some in Father's family is still difficult for me. I am constantly reminded of how selfish and critical my natural tendencies are. But the joy shared with Father when touching another with His love has a way of effectively challenging the pride that seeks its own. And now I am enjoying being part of a family of believers whose hearts are truly knit together in love.

Although we represent only a small number of those who started this journey together, the rewards are enormous. There is an abiding sense of Father's pleasure and an increasing revelation of His heart as we walk together with open hearts, hands and homes. We don't know what new challenge or unexpected blessing is waiting for us around the next bend in the road, but the warm companionship we share on the journey softens the bumps and multiplies the joys.

13

SALT AND LIGHT

"You are the salt of the earth. But if the salt loses its saltiness, how can it be made salty again?"

"You are the light of the world. A city on a hill cannot be hidden. Neither do people light a lamp and put it under a bowl. Instead they put it on its stand, and it gives light to everyone in the house. In the same way let your light shine before men, that they may see your good deeds and praise your Father in heaven."

(Matthew 5:13a, 14–16 NIV)

"You're here to be salt-seasoning that brings out God-flavors of this earth...You're here to be light, bringing out the God-colors in the world."

(The Message)

"What makes you different?"

Nancy B (not my former assistant) had finally gotten up the courage to address the singer at the upscale bar she frequented on Friday evenings. It wasn't the words in the songs he sang as he accompanied himself on the baby grand. It was something more subtle, an inexplicable sense of peace and wellbeing that his presence seemed to bring into the room. The musician looked up and smiled at the blond, blue eyed young lady standing beside his piano. "I read the Bible," was his only reply.

Nancy left the bar to search for a Bible. As a communist sympathizer actively involved in the protest movement of the day, she would be hard pressed to find a Bible among any of her friends. After securing one at a bookstore, Nancy secluded herself in her Los Gatos apartment for several days and read until her eyes were sore.

Unable to resist the conviction of the Spirit any longer, she found a church building where a meeting was being held and told someone that she wanted to "get saved." Nancy found Mobile

Ministries a few days later and has been serving the Lord ever since, with a heart ever-burning for those who have never heard the message of God's love.

Well Seasoned Christians

I wonder how many Christians see their lives as "seasoning" in the marketplace. Most young people I talk to who have a desire to be used of God lament that their job is keeping them from their higher calling! Because they view "ministry" in the context of church work, many develop an attitude toward their employment that effectively diminishes the "saltiness" factor. What would happen if they began to realize that they have been planted at their workplace or neighborhood as a God-agent to whet the appetites of their co-workers or neighbors for Him?

Few of us are gifted communicators with the sensitivity to share the good news of God's love in His perfect timing with those around us. Many would jeopardize their job if they did so. But any child of God who goes about his or her duties as worship unto the Lord, while receiving His love for others is making someone thirsty.

In the excellent book on this subject, *Church that Works*, David Oliver points out that one Hebrew word is used for both work and worship in Scripture. The book goes on to expand on the theme that God works and we are created in His image to do likewise. He proposes that most of us will express the destiny, the high calling of God, primarily through work.

This concept does not compliment the idea that professional ministry is the highest calling or the most effective way to promote the advance of the church. For the nature of salt is to dissolve as it flavors and preserve the entire realm of its influence. Leaven, a symbol in scripture of the enemy's evil, permeating influence, works the same way, deceiving many who remain unaware of his tactics. The salt, then, must remain salty and be sprinkled liberally everywhere, if the work of the enemy is to be rendered ineffective.

Jesus calls His followers light as well as salt. Although one must be seen if his light is to shine, a primarily vocal ministry is in no way implied in Christ's words. Yet it is certainly an added joy when our honesty and loving behavior open up the opportunity to share the good news with others.

Rapping for Jesus

Mike Norrise was a professing Muslim and amateur rapper when he and his fiancé came to me for pre-marriage counseling. After several sessions, he invited Jesus Christ to take over his life and began a new journey with singular passion. Several years later, Mike took a job at a school for handicapped children where he worked together with 40 other employees.

It wasn't long before they began to notice Mike's thankful attitude, his compassion for others, his promptness to forgive when wronged and the integrity which characterized his work ethics. When they learned that Mike loved the Lord, they began to ask him questions about God and the Bible at every opportunity. Finally the demands on his time made it difficult for him to concentrate on his duties, so he made an announcement. "I'm in the parking lot early studying my Bible every day before work. If you want to know more, you can meet me there a half hour before starting time." To Mike's surprise, there was a large group of employees in the parking lot to meet him the next day and each day for some time afterwards.

Mike was never encouraged to invite anyone "to church," but to teach them and baptize them himself as they came into a relationship with Christ. Too often the institution becomes the bowl under which the lamp is hid. There are thousands of folks like Mike who could be lighting up the marketplace and extending the kingdom to every corner of the earth. Instead they are hiding their light in the four walls of the institution or shining it in the face of other Christians.

Mike has since moved on to another area, but the fruit of the bright light he allowed to shine in his everyday duties remains as an example of normal church life.

Friend of Sinners

For the most part, the church of today does not understand the nature of the friendship with sinners that Jesus set as an example for us. We either become like them or separate ourselves from them. Jesus did neither. Having no part of the world in Him he feared no danger of contamination by it, but was free to eat and drink with the worst of sinners. He loved them freely and identified with their joys and sorrows while remaining independent of their influence. His relationship with them was not contrived for the purpose of winning them over to the kingdom.

Of course, He longed for all to know the Father as He did and went wherever the Spirit led Him for the express purpose of preaching the Good News to all who would take it to heart. But the bottom line was that Jesus genuinely enjoyed being with people because He loved them.

Several years before this book was written, a group of us began frequenting a large and somewhat notorious bar, called The Texas Saloon, on Friday evenings. We would play pool and darts for drinks (soft drinks for us) while getting to know the local clientele. Before that part of the evening began, we gathered in the church office to pray. On one occasion, I noticed a sense of uneasiness among the participants and asked if they were feeling guilty for playing games in a bar while seldom getting the opportunity to share Christ there. Several nods confirmed my suspicions.

"There are only two kinds of people I enjoy being with," I said. "On-fire Christians and pagans. Friday evenings have generally been nights off for me, and I like to have fun on a night off. I enjoy pool and darts and get to do it every Friday with people I enjoy. If we're not enjoying ourselves, we will probably not be very good company."

The freedom to have fun and enjoy unbelievers in the atmosphere where they were comfortable seemed to release the faith to see God work. While about 30 of us were praying in a home one evening, we sensed strongly that God was encouraging us to believe Him for the property belonging to the bar. We were reminded that if God sent us to occupy a territory for the kingdom, we could be as sure of doing so as when He instructed Joshua and the Israelites to possess the land, simply by walking on it with their ears tuned to God and their bows trained on the enemy. When we were through praying, no doubt remained. The Texas Saloon had been acquired for kingdom purposes.

Transformation!

Soon, a strange thing began to occur. Though the bar had thrived for many years, the number of customers passing through the door each evening now began to decrease on a weekly basis. We began to schedule our visits for a later hour when motorcycle gangs joined the crowd, but the numbers were steadily dwindling then as well. Losing profits at a rapid rate, the management decided to introduce topless entertainment. We concluded that our Friday night outing to that bar was over and waited to see what would happen next.

The bar continued to lose customers at a rapid rate until the owners finally decided to call it quits. They shut the doors and put the place up for sale. Several pornographic organizations attempted to buy it, but the deal always fell through. We continued to pray. Several months after the bar closed, the entire structure was leveled to the ground. Soon, new construction was underway and a large edifice began to rise quickly. Finally the day came when driving by the site I noticed a sign identifying the function of the bold new structure. Where the Texas Saloon had thrived for over 30 years, there now stands a large church facility where hundreds of Russian believers gather to worship the King.

Each year church groups in this country spend millions of dollars in an attempt to draw unbelievers into their facilities for various events designed to present them with the gospel. Yet the great majority of those "making decisions for Christ" at such events are unaccounted for several months later. The same can be said of most city-wide evangelistic crusades. This is true in spite of ever-improving follow-up programs.

Conversely, those who are attracted to Christ by the demonstration of His love through the life of one or more of His disciples are held by the love that drew them initially. This should not come as a surprise, for Jesus never exhorted His followers to try to get unbelievers to come to a gathering but rather to *be* witnesses wherever they went.*

*Some readers may want to explore the potential effectiveness of relationally-based Christianity in the context of world missions. As the author's involvement with world missions has been based on a more traditional approach until shortly before this writing, his experience is too limited to warrant a first hand observation here. However, the incredible story of Bruce Nelson and the tribal Motilonis as recorded in the fascinating book *BRUCHKO* recounts what is easily one of the most successful mission efforts ever:

Representing no organization, newly-converted 19-year-old Bruce was shot with arrows and kidnapped by the hostile tribe that he was convinced God had commissioned him to reach. How Bruce became a member of their society, demonstrated the love of Christ through their culture, and ultimately witnessed the absolute transformation of an entire people group is unforgettable high adventure. But the story doesn't end there. The Motilonis who encountered the miraculous power of the risen Christ on a regular basis went on to reach their neighboring enemy tribes until the love and power of God was made famous throughout the entire region. Although the government of Brazil presented him with an award for his work on several occasions, Bruce refused to be called the leader of the Motiloni people who were left with no choice but to seek the Lord for all decisions. No organization was ever formed nor a building ever built. Yet the Kingdom of God was dramatically established in a region and amongst a people that no organized missions group had ever been able to get close to.

This report is not intended to suggest that organized missions are necessarily ineffective. This author has personally visited a community that was transformed through the relational approach developed by Medical Ambassadors International. Team members of that organization emulate the scripturally-based method of initially connecting with a "man of peace" in a given community. Through him they are able to identify the elders of the community. Working together with the elders, the team is able to discover the felt needs of the community and then begin to educate the people on how to address the needs using locally available resources. Members of the team are trained in countless areas including water purification, food resource and production, disease prevention and cure, general education, landscaping, etc. During the five year process, which includes group discussion (never lectures), role play and various games, the community members are led to discover the answers for themselves. Ultimately, they discover the Answer through the love that is shown and the scriptural truths that are shared. At that point, the initial ministry team completes a gradual withdrawal leaving the continued development and maintenance of the community in local hands. It is then to become the goal of the transformed community to reach out to a neighboring community in the same way. Medical Ambassadors International is witnessing community transformation in well over 50 nations around the world.

Though the mission works summarized above are widely dissimilar in several obvious aspects, the similarities they do share may illustrate some fundamental keys to an effective response to the great commission. The development of long-term relationships with those receiving the gospel has been a non-optional ingredient in both examples.

Second, those bringing the good news demonstrated the love of Christ through their lives long before "preaching" it. Third, the members of the community being "reached" were led to discover solutions and to take the leadership in the application of such. Finally, the community was recognized as a priesthood of believers, answerable to God rather than to an outside organization.

14

KINGDOM CITIES

"It simply doesn't work!" Jim's dark eyes reflected the frustration he was feeling as he placed his tray on the table across from me. "For all these years I have taught my heart out, used every available method to facilitate communication and have done everything I know to build a relationally-based church group. Yet New Testament Christianity is still not a reality among us." Jim paused and searched my face as he reached for a muffin.

I had met Jim many years ago when he became involved in a monthly meeting of pastors that was initiated with the vision of working toward unity in the greater Sacramento area. Two or three dozen leaders gathered to share needs, pray for one another and for the city. Eventually five of us functioned as a facilitation team to maintain order and direction for the larger group. As part of that team, Jim was appreciated for his upbeat attitude, childlike transparency and sensitivity to hidden agendas. Throughout the years he and I had come to trust one another.

"Pastoring is all about two issues", Jim continued, "power and money. The truth is, I've had it. I'm ready to resign."

Although Jim's story matched my own experience, I was somewhat surprised that he had reached this point. Extremely busy with the responsibilities of pastoring a large congregation and heading up world missions for his denomination, he seemed to thrive on the fast-paced lifestyle that resulted.

As I began to share with Jim some of the truths that were beginning to change the way we thought about "church" and to impact the way we functioned as a group, something began to come to life within him. Soon Jim began to walk in new understanding during the next several months and the process of transition started in the group of people he walks with.

But while Jim was experiencing a resurgence of new life in his situation, progress toward unity in the city remained at a standstill. Differing viewpoints and philosophies in three vital areas seemed to produce a stalemate to forward progress.

The first issue touched the tension between *being* and *doing*. Some felt that we were called together to develop strategy involving city-wide outreach programs and evangelistic crusades. They were convinced that evangelism was the key to reaching the city. Others believed that relationship and concerted prayer was the foundation for transformation. The latter insisted that effective evangelism was the caboose rather than the engine.

Filling Creation with God

In the book *Church that Works* author James Thwaites makes a poignant observation that touches these two issues. He writes: *"...powerful prayer rises from powerful relationships, and powerful relationships come from strong engagement with the work, in line with the divine purpose in that sphere of work."* It is important to note that Thwaites is not talking about evangelistic programs or events when he uses the word *work*. He is referring to the various means of employment in which God has placed His people to be salt and light. If spiritual leaders would recognize that the church is to fill all creation with the fullness of the Godhead (Eph. 1:22–23) through the saints in their assigned place of duty, they would serve them in fulfilling God's purpose for their workplace. The author asserts that when leaders believe in what the saints are doing and affirm the importance of their calling in the workplace by serving them toward their goals, strong relationship grows from the powerful agreement established. From that place of agreement springs prayer that solicits the presence and power of God.

Perhaps if spiritual leaders were to agree concerning this priority and pray together toward the goals stated above, a beginning point of unity among leaders could be achieved. Leaders in the workplace would be included in the strategy planning and prayer meetings. The focus would shift from finding ways to solicit the involvement of the saints in evangelistic programs to equipping them in kingdom principles and strategy for their workplace.

This brings us to the second area that challenged the progress of our little pastor's group. Everyone agreed that we were to equip the saints and release them into their callings. But our understanding of "release" and "calling" were worlds apart. Most of the leaders still considered the members of the congregation they pastored as *their* sheep. They needed to keep them close so that they would embrace the "vision of the house" and grow under their protection and supervision.

To release them meant that they would be allowed to function in their gifts under authority and within the context of the pastor's vision. Their calling was defined in the context of how their "ministry work" built up the local body they attended.

Once again, I will draw on the insight of Mr. Thwaites. He writes: *"If our release is conditional, then it is not release. There is a time for nurture and there is a time for release."*

In those days I would have been in unqualified agreement with Mr. Thwaites. Today I do not believe that we *ever* have the right to hold on to the people with whom God has privileged us to walk. Obviously, if one is not restrained, he needs no release. But I believe wholeheartedly that there is a season where those younger in the Lord draw from the wisdom of the more mature before venturing further into more challenging stretches of the journey. Even then, the insight of some who have gone before them will always remain a resource to them. But as leaders, we must never expect them to return to build "our vision." I like the way Thwaites puts it in another place: *"We must, as leaders, keep dispersing resources and no longer be kept busy accumulating and managing them."*

My Church or One Church?

When we are focused on "accumulating and managing" people, our vision remains self-centered rather than kingdom-centered. We find ourselves too busy to lend our time and energy to a vision that encompasses the whole city. The larger implication suggests that our priorities are not consistent with God's heart for whole cities and even nations. Yet most of us in our pastors group were consumed with the local expression that continued to define the context of our ministries. Thus, the third area impeding our feeble attempt at unity was our lack of understanding or willingness to accept the concept of one church in the city.

It is significant that Jesus mentioned the word "church" only three times while referring to the kingdom of God 79 times. Paul, the apostle, mentioned the word more often but defined it as God's people in a particular city. He addressed his letters "to the church of God in Corinth," "to the church of the Thessalonians" or "to all the saints" in (one city or another). He does mention the *churches* in Galatia, but that was a province with several cities. He instructs Timothy to appoint (recognize) elders in every city. In fact, every reference to the church we can find in New Testament scriptures and early church history recognizes only one church in any city where God's people were established. The implications of this are obvious. The evil of a competitive spirit or the tendency to compare was not possible, nor could the church "steel sheep" from itself. Rather, the church was one people with one purpose and one vision for one city.

Yet today we have localized the concept of church to the degree that each gathering place seeks to be distinguished from other groups by its alleged superior worship, teaching, or unique emphasis. And since the understanding of church has been reduced to indicate a building where Christian activity is centralized, the size and architectural virtues of the facility itself become a comparative value. The resulting fragmentation of the present day church makes the concept of unity appear as an impossible dream while the society we are called to impact with the gospel remains largely unreached.

Apostolic Comparison

Presently there is a great emphasis in many ecclesiastical circles on apostles and apostolic ministry. "Apostolic" networks are being formed at a rapid rate with an "apostle" at their helm. A leader is generally recognized as an apostle if he has planted a significant number of churches or formed a network of recognized ministries that look to him for leadership.

It is doubtful whether several of the New Testament apostles would have qualified to function in their gifting under these standards as they neither planted churches nor formed networks. What they did do was equip the saints for the works of service.

If Paul's criteria for identifying an apostle are accurate, we can assume that all of the apostles performed signs and wonders. We know that most of them were martyred for spreading the gospel. Not one of them built cathedrals, formed networks or strove to gain a following. When believers at Corinth began to identify with certain apostles which resulted, predictably, in jealousy and bickering, Paul soundly rebuked them. He asked them if Christ were divided and called them "worldly" and "mere infants in Christ." He went on to say that Paul and Apollos were only servants but that (the saints at Corinth) were God's building.

A cursory examination of the scriptures makes it evident that true apostolic ministry is characterized, among other things, by selfless leaders who suffered tremendous hardship for the furtherance of the gospel and the growth of the saints. A good percentage of the epistles were given to the subject of harmony among the saints as they were instructed to walk in love, forgiveness, humility and unity.

Perhaps if modern day apostolic ministers were focused less on building organizations and followings and more on building God's kingdom indiscriminate of personal gain, unity in the church of a given city would follow as a natural result. Those who have viewed the *Transformation* videos will remember that in every case where a city was significantly changed by the power of God, the believers in that city had become desperate enough to lay aside religious bias and style to seek God together as one people for His intervention.

Still, wherever any genuine effort is made towards fulfilling God's heart in a given area He seems eager to affirm it with His blessing.

Blessing of Unity

At one point in our pastor's group, the "prayers" and "doers" both agreed that it seemed good to plan a multi-church baptism in the American River. On the Sunday afternoon of the event, a couple thousand believers from twelve local fellowships gathered on a grassy shore where the river widened and the current slowed.

The gathering happened to be in the same area where, shortly before the gold rush, an evangelist preached to the merchants guiding cargo boats as they steamed into the newly-born city of Sacramento to deliver their goods.

Toward the middle of the river, several pleasure crafts idled in the doldrums as their passengers partied and observed the growing gathering with curiosity. Soon a several-hundred-voice Russian choir began singing hymns as the crowd lifted their collective voice in worship. After several pastors prayed, a guest speaker from one of the fellowships gave a powerful message on the cross of Christ. As the ample sound system carried his words across the water, the posture of those on the party boats indicated that they were listening intently. But the evidence of God's presence was the most obvious as the baptisms began to take place simultaneously all along that 500 yard stretch of river.

Suddenly all three of one party boat's passengers dove into the water and began swimming toward us. Soon other onlookers descended from their observation point on the bridge and came into the water as well. These newcomers wanted to be saved and baptized on the spot. Most of them probably never would have entered a church building, but on that one day they witnessed a church without walls! They didn't care who baptized them or what building they met in. They only knew what they saw and heard. They felt the presence of God who, like them, didn't care who baptized them or what building they met in. Of course He *always* sees a church without walls.

Imagine what could happen if all the "church" groups in a given city made the choice to discard everything that hindered them from moving together as one church. Christians everywhere are praying and waiting for God to send revival. Could it be that God is waiting for us?

Epilogue

It is my hope that in these few pages I have been able to inspire some to explore beyond the traditional understanding of church life. Perhaps you have been able to peek briefly through a window that has never been open to you before. It may have frightened you a bit or may even have made you angry, but if you are reading these closing thoughts, you are most likely hungry for more than has been offered here. If so, this little book was worth writing.

I don't pretend to have all, or even most, of the answers concerning what has been discussed here. I have refrained from exploring most of the principles in-depth that have been touched on in this writing for fear of intellectualizing that which I have not yet applied. For me, the journey has just begun.

Certainly there is no single method or "how to" formula for transitioning from organized 'church' to a more relational approach to life in the family of God. The same can be said concerning reaching the lost or bringing the fruit of unity to a city or, for that matter, any other dynamic discussed in this writing.

This book is not an advertisement for the house church "movement" or any other so-called movement that may be gaining notoriety today. The word "movement" generally tends to describe man's effort to harness and ultimately control something that God initiated to bring His people into greater freedom in Christ. It is not about *where* we meet or *how* we "do" church. Rather, I have sought to touch on several truths that may help some become disentangled from the false promises and ultimate bondage produced by religion so that they may live in the love, joy and freedom that Father intended for His family on earth.

A Wonderful Reality

A wonderful truth about our relationship with Father is that He treats every one of us so individually. And He made each one unique because He relishes having a relationship with you that He has never enjoyed with anyone else throughout all of time. We must not let anyone or any system interfere with such a rare and sacred engagement.

He has given us His Holy Spirit to lead us into all truth. Jesus said that the Holy Spirit would take the things that are His and His Father's and will make them known to us. We can trust Him to lead each of us in the way that He has prepared specifically for each of us.

His goal for every one of us while we are on this planet is to be conformed into the image of

His Son. Only Father knows exactly what process He will use to accomplish this in your life, but the love relationship with Him that will grow through it will overcome the pain.

I have no idea what waits around the next corner on the path this little group of pilgrims is traveling on. We have found others in the city who are on a similar journey and have expressed the desire to walk together. Perhaps a day will come when those who have traded religion for relationship are received as servants to folks who are hungering for more of Christ. Nevertheless, those who truly follow Christ will always consider themselves aliens in a foreign land. Abraham lived in tents because he was looking for a city with foundations, meaning that as an alien to this world, he had no attachments here. The writer of Hebrews tells us that God was not ashamed to be called the God of those who confessed such things. Surely this is the key to real faith, for if we identify with this world, we cannot exercise the faith that is reserved for those who represent only the kingdom of heaven.

Rooted in Love

Later we read that a time will come when God will shake both the heavens and the earth until only that which cannot be shaken will remain. We are told that we are receiving a kingdom that cannot be shaken and are exhorted to be thankful and to worship God acceptably with reverence and awe. We are reminded that our God is a consuming fire. And then we are told to "keep on loving each other as brothers."

And that last statement, I believe, is the key to the kingdom. We are encouraged in Ephesians to be "rooted and grounded in love." It is the kingdom of love that cannot be shaken. The only ground in which we are to put down roots is in the vineyard of relationship where our loving Father is the caretaker.

I wonder what will happen to the beautiful buildings and religious systems when the great shaking comes. Certainly what man has created will not remain. But those who are consumed with love for Christ and His bride will not be consumed by the fire of God. Only by His grace are we able ever to know such love, and because of His grace we shall.

* * *

It was definitely God's grace that took the form of the two Samoan men who found me crouching in pain on the lava bed. I slipped the flip flops onto my bruised feet and was filled with gratitude for this timely provision so desperately needed. As I made my way easily down the wash bed toward the previously arranged rendezvous point,

I mused over the events that led to my perilous adventure.

When I first stood with the tourists at the base of the falls in the Hawaiian rain forest, I felt cheated. Was this the big attraction? A group of people staring at tons of water as it crashed noisily onto the canyon floor? It wasn't as though the cascading falls failed to present a captivating sight. And the thunderous roar it created was quite impressive. But there was no way to interact with the unchanging scene before me. I wanted more. I wanted to engage the beautiful and dramatic environment surrounding me, to discover the source of the falls. But I was boxed in by canyon walls and a sign denying access. So I set off into forbidden territory in hopes of satisfying the burning desire within. I ended up finding a bit more than I had bargained for, but in the process I learned some valuable lessons.

This has been the story of some ordinary folks who have shaken off the binding influence of religious obligation to discover the hidden treasures and joys of a free life in Christ. Coming into this liberty is an ongoing process as challenging and sometimes painful as my descent from the top of the falls. Some of the difficulties have been shared here; others are yet to be borne.

But for me, the rewards far outweigh the cost. I am beginning to realize a freedom from the tyranny of false expectations, religious obligation, and impossible standards imposed by myself and others. I am discovering the joy of loving people without trying to change them. And I'm growing in the understanding of how boundless His love truly is. Such love provides the security I need to be more child-like in trusting Father for the needs of each day.

It has also provided an escape from the confines of the "box canyon" created by my narrow views of God and the boundaries I thought He had set for me.

Dreams that Come True

I used to dream about what I would like to do if I wasn't a "pastor." I envisioned writing books and producing and acting in movies that would encourage and challenge believers and reach out to those searching. However, I dismissed those dreams as mere fantasies serving to distract me from the more conventional form of ministry that consumed my time and energy.

Recently, I sensed that God was encouraging me to pursue my dreams; that it was He who had planted them in my heart. Now several of us with like-vision are in the beginning stages of developing a multi-media production company with a mission to present Christ to all who are hungering for a real and simple relationship with their creator.

Others have also found the freedom to pursue their dreams. They are learning that God uses unexpected avenues through which to demonstrate His creativity when they are willing to remove the boundaries often set by their misconception of His ways. It's always a bit frightening for anyone to climb out of the familiar ruts of tradition and launch out into uncharted territory. Yet a whole new world seems to come alive in a fresh way when we do. And Father is always present with His affirmation and provision.

Only a small group remains of those that began this journey together several years ago. Still, many of us share a growing anticipation for future days yet unfolding. Though we are fewer in number, God seems so much bigger than when we first set out to discover His purposes for us as a congregation! Our own limitations no longer present an obstacle in the face of His super-abundant grace and overflowing love. And each small step we make with our hand in His occasions another encounter with the glory of His presence.

Yes, the path is still perilous at times, but we are secure in Father's love. And the thrill of discovery, the sweet air of freedom and the joy of being family provide but a taste of what certainly must be waiting just around the next bend in the trail.

Comparison Chart #1

Institutional Mindset	Relational Thinking
Programs	Relationship-based priorities
Leadership Authority	Authority of every believer
Building-centered focus	People centered
Sunday A.M. is the main event	Any gathering of 2 or more
Attending meetings is a high priority.	Serving others takes a higher priority.
Attractional (how can we get the lost to come to us?)	Incarnational (Christ living through us)

Comparison Chart #2

Living in Christ	'Doing Church'*
Presenting oneself to God in every circumstance	Holding rededication service or altar call
Praising at all times	Worship Service
Praying unceasingly	Prayer meeting
Meditating on the Word day and night	Church service or devotional time
Sharing the Word as the Spirit leads.	Planned sermon or evangelistic service.
Witness by lifestyle and Spirit-prompted sharing	Outreach event or program

*I am not intending to express my disfavor with every item on the "Doing Church" list. I often participate in and enjoy corporate gatherings where worship and praise, prayer and even an occasional "planned sermon" is shared. And nothing is more satisfying to me than those intimate times alone with Father that some call "devotions." It is when planned events become a substitute for daily living in Father's love that they cease to be life-giving.

Appendix I

REFERENCES

Chapter 1

Matthew 23:25–26; Isaiah 1:14, 29:13a
Jeremiah 2:13; Revelation 3:14–16,22

Chapter 2

Jeremiah 31:21; Galatians 1:10

Chapter 3

Matthew 20:25–28; Luke 22:25–26;
Matthew 23:8–12

Chapter 4

Ephesians 3:14–15; 1Peter 2:9a; Jeremiah 5:31;
Galatians 5:1–6

Chapter 5

1Corinthians 4:9–10; 2Corinthians 4:7;
John 19:26–27

Chapter 6

1Corinthians 14:26–31; Acts 20:7

Chapter 7

Hebrews 10:25; Matthew 18:20

Chapter 8

Matthew 16:13–23; Matthew 17:1–5; Isaiah 10:27

Chapter 9

Hebrews 12:2

Chapter 10

Psalm 62:1–2; Psalm 63:3,7–8; 1Corinthians 12:21

Chapter 11

Ephesians 3:14–19; Romans 12:5; Matthew 6:33;
1John 4:20; Colossians 2:2–3

Chapter 12

Matthew 5:13a,14–16

Chapter 13

Romans 1:7; 1Corinthians 1:2; 1Corinthians
3:1–9; 2Corinthians 1:1; Galatians 1:2;
1Thessalonians 1:1; 2Thessalonians 1:1;
1Corinthians 1:12–13; Ephesians1:22–23

Epilogue

Hebrews 11:9–10,13,16; Hebrews 12:26–13:1;
Ephesians 3:17

Appendix II

BIBLIOGRAPHY

Chapter 4

Jacobsen, Wayne, *Body Life, Lifestream.org,* December 2002

Chapter 7

Thwaites, James, *Renegotiating the Church Contract: the death and the life of the 21st century church,* Paternoster Press, 2002

Chapter 12

Oliver, David, *Church that Works,* Milton Keynes: Word

Olson, Bruce, *Bruchko,* YWAM Publishing www. ywampublishing.com

Chapter 13

Otis, Jr., George, *Transformations,* The Sentinel Group, 1999

FURTHER READING

Jacobsen, Wayne, *The Naked Church*, BodyLife Publishers, 1998

Order at www.lifestream.org

Lund, Robert A., *The Way Church Ought To Be,* Outside the Box Press, 2001

Email info@nogarbagebooks.com

Viola, Frank, *Rethinking the Wineskin,* Present Testimony Ministry

Order at www.ptmin@aol.com

Viola, Frank, *Who is Your Covering?* Present Testimony Ministry, 2001

Order at www.ptmin@aol.com

About the Author

David Fredrickson was a pastor for almost 30 years and has traveled the world preaching, teaching and training church leaders. In 2001 a fresh understanding of life in God's family moved him to begin a journey that has become the subject of this book. He is currently writing for Family Room Media and is helping people to come into the freedom of the Father's love. David and his wife Rachel reside in Citrus Heights, California.

CHURCH OUTSIDE THE WALLS is the first documentary to explore church life outside of organized religion. Hosted by David Fredrickson, this four part series gets close-up and personal in candid interviews with former pastors and congregation members who explain why they left and what they've discovered. Part 2 examines the historical evolution of organized religion and positional authority. Part 3 explores the dynamics of church as family. Finally, Part 4 speculates on what might lie ahead for the church in future days. Here, the viewer is invited along on a tour of non-traditional and innovative expressions of church life with a missional emphasis.

Part 1, The Drop-outs is **now available.** Who are they? Why did they leave? What have they discovered? Their answers may surprise you.

Visit www.familyroommedia.com for preview and ordering information.

This and other quality books are available from

OverLookedBooks

Visit us online at:
www.overlookedbooks.com

Printed in the United States
56132LVS00004B/382-504